FEEDBACK

Essential writing skills
for intermediate students

Jane Sherman

OXFORD UNIVERSITY PRESS

Oxford University Press

Great Clarendon Street, Oxford OX2 6DP

Oxford New York
Athens Auckland Bangkok Bogota Bombay
Buenos Aires Calcutta Cape Town Dar es Salaam Delhi
Florence Hong Kong Istanbul Karachi Kuala Lumpur
Madras Madrid Melbourne Mexico City Nairobi
Paris Singapore Taipei Tokyo Toronto Warsaw

and associated companies in
Berlin Ibadan

Oxford and *Oxford English*
are trade marks of Oxford University Press

ISBN 0 19 454289 0 (Italian edition)
ISBN 0 19 454277 7 (International edition)

© Oxford University Press 1994

First published 1994
Fourth impression 1997

Typeset by Tradespools Ltd, Frome, Somerset
Printed in Italy

Acknowledgements

The illustrations in this book are by:
Oxford Illustrators (handwriting, pages 112,
113, 114, 115);
Philippa Parkinson (pages 24, 25, 35, 50, 63,
78, 91, 101, 104, 131, 145);
Alex Tiani (pages 11, 18, 29, 42, 57, 71, 73, 86,
98, 111, 125, 127, 139, 149, 152);
Harry Venning (pages 32, 39, 40, 82, 112, 113,
114, 115).
Cover illustration: *Drawing Hands* - 1948, by
M.C. Escher (1898-1972). © M.C. Escher
Foundation - Baarn - Holland.

Photo on page 92 by Geoffrey Biddle.

The Publisher and Author would like to thank
the following for their kind permission to use
articles, extracts or adaptations from copyright
material:
Climbing the Stairs by Margaret Powell, Pan,
reproduced by permission of Tody Eady
Associates Ltd; *A Streetcar Named Desire*,
Signet Books © 1947 Tennessee Williams,
reprinted by permission of The Lady St Just and
John L. Eastman, Trustees under the Will of
Tennessee Williams; © Milo O. Frank 1986,
extracted from *How To Get Your Point Across
In 30 Seconds Or Less* published by Transworld
Publishers Ltd, all rights reserved; extract on
asparagus, *Guardian Weekly,* © The Guardian
1990; 'Beware the Eurogook' by Sylvia Chalker,
'Migrants to start profanity course', 'Golden
Bull Winners', published by *EFL Gazette*, 10
Wrights Lane, London W8 6TA; *Six Thinking
Hats* by Edward de Bono, Viking 1986,
copyright © Mica Management Resources Inc.
1985; 'The Hurled Ashtray' from *Crazy Salad*
by Nora Ephron, Alfred A. Knopf Inc. 1972,
reprinted by permission of International
Creative Management Inc., copyright 1972 by
Nora Ephron; extract from *Our Unalienable
Rights* by R. G. Storey, 1965, courtesy of
Charles C. Thomas, Publisher, Springfield,
Illinois; 'The Fun They Had', from *Earth is
Room Enough* by Isaac Asimov copyright © by
Isaac Asimov used by permission of Doubleday,
a division of Bantam Doubleday Dell Publishing
Group, Inc.

Every effort has been made to trace the owners
of copyright material in this book, but we
should be pleased to hear from any copyright
owner whom we have been unable to contact in
order to rectify any errors or omissions.

Acknowledgement

In writing this book I have drawn widely on my experience of teaching students of the Facoltà di Magistero at Rome University, La Sapienza, and elsewhere. The examples, illustrations and models in particular owe much to my students, and I am grateful to them all.

Dedication

*This course is dedicated to Hilda Feld,
because it was all I had to give at the time.*

CONTENTS

		Language Preparation	Writing Tutorial

Introduction
Page 8

Preliminary Work
Page 11

For and against compositions

1 **Presentation**
Page 14

Uncountables
Time, money and problems
Prepositions   Spelling

Document presentation requirements

2 **Your voice**
Page 26

Narrative past
Use of far, far away
Prepositions   Punctuation

Having something to say
Keeping a writer's diary

3 **Criteria**
Page 39

each other
Kinds of *knowing*
Prepositions   Spelling

Evaluating writing - one's own and others'

4 **Using Feedback**
Page 54

Zero article
Enabling
Prepositions   Punctuation

Getting and using teacher feedback

5 **Paragraphing**
Page 68

Future possibilities
now, soon and *recently*
Prepositions   Spelling

The form and purpose of paragraphing

6 **What to say**
Page 81

most, all and *some*
People and their kids
Prepositions   Punctuation

A procedure for getting and selecting ideas

7 **Style**
Page 95

Speech to writing
Emphasis
Prepositions
Spelling

A semi-formal style and what to avoid

8 **Pinning it down**
Page 107

Contrasts
Biodata
Prepositions   Punctuation

Examples, illustrations and particulars

9 **Organization (1)**
Page 122

Genitive
Economics and politics
Prepositions   Spelling

Beginnings, endings and avoiding rambling

10 **Organization (2)**
Page 135

Connections   Opinions
Prepositions   Punctuation

Grouping and classifying points

Language tests
Page 149

Teacher's notes
Page 155

Key to language tests
Page 173

Key to units
Page 174

Assignment *P = Planning*	Reader Feedback	Diary	Reading
Writing experience	Reacting to content		
Money *P: Making notes*	Layout Content		*Money* Attitudes to money Questionnaire
An important day *P: Notes and focus*	Layout Content	An object	*First day off* Looking for adventure Autobiography
Working people *P: Details and* *endings*	Layout Strong points Content	Animals	*Babe Secoli* A supermarket checker Transcribed speech
Virtues and vices *P: Making* *connections*	Layout Form Strong points	Annual report	*A streetcar named Desire* Tensions and teasing Playscript
Campaign *P: Selecting and* *shaping ideas*	Layout Form and paragraphs Content	Favourite films	*Beware the Eurogook* Report on the Plain English Campaign (magazine article)
Choice of subjects *P: Generating ideas*	Layout Form and paragraphs Range and accuracy	Photograph	*The Green Hat* Creative thinking Exposition and exhortation
Language *P: Generating and* *selecting ideas*	Layout Form Style Content	Foreigners	*Jargon and slang* Bureaucratese, swearing, colloquial language Miscellany
The life of women *P: Finding good* *illustrations*	Layout Form Illustration Content	Superstition	*The hurled ashtray* Behaviour towards women Personal column
Injustice *P: Pinning down an* *abstract idea*	Layout Form Purpose Style Content	Conflict (dialogue)	*Testimony* Constructing a point Courtroom questioning
Education *P: Timing in exams*	All criteria	Advice (open letter)	*The fun they had* Education in the future Short story

FEEDBACK COURSE RECORD

Unit	Write	Tick when you have:			
	Date completed	used teacher's feedback	done Language Preparation	written assignment	got reader's feedback
Introduction					
Unit 1					
Unit 2					
Unit 3					
Unit 4					
Unit 5					
Unit 6					
Unit 7					
Unit 8					
Unit 9					
Unit 10					

Write what you have learnt from:		Leave this space for the teacher to write his/her comment
reader's feedback	ideas in the unit	

INTRODUCTION

Helping you improve your writing

What this course is for

This course is to help you improve your writing, in particular your writing of compositions and essays.

Students often do not know what is expected of them when they write in English. This course will tell you what is expected, and why, and help you to practise it.

We think this course will give you a lot more confidence and a lot more pleasure in writing and that your progress will be visible to you.

What this course is NOT for

This is not a language course. It does not set out to improve your listening or speaking, or to teach you all the grammar or vocabulary you should know (although you will learn quite a lot of both grammar and vocabulary). For these you should be following a complete language course which deals with all aspects of the language.

What you will need

To get the most out of this course, you should have:

- a good easy-to-use reference grammar
- a good bilingual dictionary
- a good English-English learner's dictionary.

Do not assume that what you have is good enough. Ask your teacher for some advice about what is on the market, and also use your own common sense. A reference grammar is useless if you don't understand it. A dictionary is no good if it doesn't have the information you need.

How to use this course

There are several ways this course can be used:

- **Individually** You may be working through it individually, seeing a tutor after each assignment. If this is the case, you may find it easier if there are two of you: see if you can find a friend who also wants to do it.

- **Writing workshop** You may be following a writing workshop, where everyone is working in the same place at the same time, but at their own pace.

– **In class** Your teacher may be using it in class and asking you to do parts of it for homework.

People you need

However you are using it, you do need some people to help you:

– **Teacher/tutor** One is your tutor or teacher, who will correct your English, discuss your work with you and help you to evaluate it.

– **Readers** The other is a reader – someone who will read your assignments and react to them. There are instructions for the reader in each part of the course.

    You can have the same reader each time or a different one. Choose them with care. Obviously you want someone who will be nice about your work – but at the same time you don't want someone who never says anything useful.

    If you are working with others, they will also ask you to read their work. This will develop your critical sense and will certainly make your own writing better. It should also be enjoyable!

What the course consists of

Explanation and exercises

Each unit of the course explains one main point and practises it in tasks. Some of the exercises have 'right answers' and these are given in the Key (**0–n**).

Assignment

At the end of each unit there is an assignment: a composition to write. The assignment has three supports:

1 a short section on planning
2 instructions for your reader
3 a reading text.

Language work and language tests

Before each unit there is some preparatory language work. You can do this at any time before you write the assignment for the unit.

    You can even leave it out if you do not have very much time. But before you decide to neglect it, find out if you need it. The language tests at the back of the book test the main grammar/structure and vocabulary points taught in each unit. Use the tests to diagnose your weak points and decide what you need to practise.

Record sheet

At the beginning of this book there is a record sheet which is to be filled in as you complete each unit of the course. It helps you to see how far you have got, gives information to your tutor/teacher about your reactions, and provides a space for him/her to write a general comment on each assignment.

    We suggest you make a copy of the record sheet, fill it in as you complete the units and hand it in with each assignment.

Writing and reading

The reading texts are important. They have various purposes: to put you in the mood for writing, to fill your head with English, to give you some feeling of how good writers write, to raise some questions about the subject of the assignment. To be honest, what matters is not these particular texts, but simply *doing a lot of reading in English* while you practise writing.

Writing is output. What is in your head comes out onto paper. But you can't have output without input. Words have to go into your head and learn to live there before they can come out.

If you are reading English at the same time as you are practising writing, you have the maximum possibility of increasing the amount of language you can use. Without even knowing it, you will pick up words and expressions from what you read and use them in your writing. So your writing will improve much faster if you are doing some reading too.

! ## BEFORE YOU GO ON

Complete this part and discuss it with your teacher or tutor.

What essential reference books have you got? Give their titles and publishers:

_____

_____

What reference books do you still need?

_____

_____

If you are working individually, complete this part as well and show it to your tutor:

Are you working alone or with a friend?   _____

Have you got a reader?   _____

How fast do you plan to work?
a   one unit a week   b   one unit a month   c   other   _____

Are you already reading a lot in English?   _____

! *If you meet a word you don't know you should look it up in a dictionary. Try and memorize some of these words.*

Preliminary work

What is the point of writing compositions?

If you have not asked this question already, you should do so right away.

Arguments against

Start with the arguments *against*. There are some good ones. Think of at least two strong, valid arguments against writing compositions – compositions in general, or English compositions in particular. Consult with others if you wish.

_____

_____

Arguments in favour

Now try equally hard to think of two good arguments *in favour of* learning to write compositions in English, or in any language.

_____

_____

Before you go on, discuss the arguments on both sides. Decide if you think they are strong or weak arguments, and whether you agree with them.

Some of the arguments

Arguments against

There are several good reasons for *not* writing compositions.
- **Who writes compositions?** They don't at first sight have much market value. No one in your future working life will ever ask you to write a 'composition'. You may have to write letters or reports but not compositions.
- **Writing phobia** You may dislike writing or find it boring. This is a strong argument, but it needs investigating. If you dislike writing, why do you dislike it? Do you have a good reason, or is it simply a phobia, like fear of spiders – or a block, because you feel you are not good at it?
- **It's difficult** You may find writing in English difficult. This really is not a very good argument. Everything is difficult until you have had some practice.
- **What is the point?** You write a composition, your teacher reads it, and that's the end of that. What is it all for? This is a very good question!

Arguments in favour

There are quite a lot of answers to this question, and some are better than others.
- **The exam** You have to write compositions for an exam or to get a mark in class. This is a powerful reason – but not a sufficient one. By itself, it really isn't a good enough reason for doing this course.

- **You learn to write** What you learn in writing compositions is also useful for other forms of writing. You learn to write in the semi-formal tone appropriate to reports and formal letters, to organize your subject-matter, to make your meaning clear. All these are necessary in most forms of writing.
- **It improves your English** There is no doubt, too, that regular writing of any kind is wonderful for improving your command of a second language. You have time to find the words to say what you need; you get practice in formulating phrases and sentences; you get your mistakes corrected visibly, so that you can see where you went wrong.

Why compositions?

First, because compositions are not just academic exercises, they have a real-life equivalent, the article. It is articles which fill newspapers and magazines; many radio and TV programmes are basically articles read aloud. If you ever write anything professionally in the future it is as likely to be an article as anything else.

Why do people read and write articles anyway?

Compositions are an outstanding way of communicating your personal thoughts, perceptions, experience, knowledge, feelings and ideas, of saying what you want to say. Compositions are a means of exploring and expressing yourself.

There is really nothing like writing for expressing yourself. You can speak at length – at greater length than in any normal discussion. You can find the way to make yourself clear – clearer than you can in spontaneous speech. You can work out what you really think – in a conversation you don't have time. In writing you extend yourself.

Reader's feedback

Very few writers write entirely for themselves. They need an audience. And indeed we believe that composition is a way of developing a public voice. It is a pity to waste a good composition on only one reader – your tutor or teacher – who is in any case usually concerned with evaluating it rather than simply enjoying it. This is why we have made extra readers an important part of this course.

Priorities

These are our five reasons for writing compositions. If you have others, add them.

For exams or for class requirements   _____

To improve writing in general   _____

To improve your English   _____

To learn to write articles   _____

To express yourself   _____

_____   _____

_____   _____

Now prioritize these reasons by numbering them in order of importance 1, 2, 3, etc. If possible, discuss your ranking with others.

PRELIMINARY WRITING

This is not your first assignment: it is just an opportunity to tell your tutor/ teacher about your relationship with writing in general and with writing in English in particular. Say what you want to say, not what you think your teacher wants to hear. Make it clear and legible.

> *Write a few words about your experience of writing. Use the questions below to help you. You need not follow the order of the questions.*
>
> *Have you done a lot of writing in your own language?*
> *What about writing in English?*
> *What experience do you have of this?*
> *Do you think writing in English is different from writing in your own language? How?*
>
> *Do you like writing? Why? Why not?*
> *Do you like some kinds of writing more than others? Which?*
>
> *Do you think you write well – or do you think you could write well? What are your strong points?*
> *What qualities do you think you need to be a good writer?*
>
> *What difficulties do you have with writing?*
> *What are your weak points?*
>
> *Why do you want to do this course?*

Before you hand this in, give it to a reader together with the following instructions.

FEEDBACK

To the reader

Please read the writing and write down *your immediate reactions* to the content (not to the language) in the box below. You may want to ask questions, compare experience, or agree or disagree – but do not make negative criticisms.

IMMEDIATE REACTIONS

_____

_____

_____

_____

1 Language Preparation

! **Look at Tests A and B for Unit 1, pages 149 and 152.**

Uncountables

Some words – for example, *milk*, *love*, *rubbish* – are called **uncountable** in grammar. If you are not sure about this idea, consult an expert or a grammar book.

Many languages have **countable** and **uncountable** nouns. The only problem is when **countable** words in one language are **uncountable** in another.

In English there are some **uncountable** words which are **countable** in other languages. Some of the commonest are:

work	furniture	information	hair
advice	accommodation	news	rubbish
equipment	machinery	transport	money

Point one

Uncountable nouns cannot be singular or plural. This means that you cannot use:

- the plural ending *s*
- *a/an*
- **any** word that implies number.

OK	**NOT OK**
rubbish	*a rubbish*
some rubbish	*rubbishes*
	many rubbish

Several words (like *many*) imply number and therefore cannot be used with uncountable nouns. Others can.

1 Decide which of the words below can be used with uncountables and write the uncountable noun *rubbish* after them, as in the example.

Example a quantity of *rubbish*

either _____	one _____	a little _____
a lot of _____	two _____	not much _____
each _____	very little _____	all _____
every _____	another _____	some _____
more _____	enough _____	both _____
several _____	a few _____	plenty of _____
a number of _____		

Point two

If you want to talk about a **unit** of something which is uncountable, you can sometimes say *a piece of*, e.g. *a piece of rubbish, a piece of information*.
You can do this with *information, advice, news, work, equipment* and *furniture*.
However, you only use *a piece of* when it's really necessary to talk about units.
Otherwise you avoid it.

Try using some of these words. Put in any other words you need, but as few as possible. The first one is done for you.

information **Example** This is extremely interesting *information*.

    a I'd like _____ _____, please.

    b That's a very useful _____ _____.

advice   c Can you give me _____?

    d That's an excellent _____.

    e Your _____ would be very welcome.

    f He gave me several good _____.

equipment   g Our greatest need is for _____.

    h In fact we have too _____ _____.

    i This is a very valuable _____.

work   j She lives too much for _____.

    k This is an excellent _____.

    l I have several _____ to do.

Time, money and problems

Point one

Spending, wasting and *saving* are things you can do with time or money (note that we don't say *lose* time, but *waste* it). They are useful words so it is worth learning to use them correctly. There are two things you should know:

1   The usual preposition with *spend, waste* and *save* is **on**.

    *Don't waste your time **on** him!*

    *If we go on foot we'll save **on** petrol.*

    *I'm sure I spent too much **on** this computer.*

2   As you know, you can spend (or waste) time or money **on** *things* or **on** *people*. You can also spend or waste time **on** *activities*. Here you usually use the **-ing** form of the verb.

    *I wasted two hours **trying** to find a chemist's that was open on Sundays.*
    *Spend a few minutes **thinking** about your health.*

Look at this construction:

*waste (time) **trying** (to do something)*
*spend (time) **thinking** (about something)*

To practise these, answer the questions below. If possible, swap the information with a partner. Try to use the preposition *on* or the construction with *-ing*.

a   How much time do you *spend* doing these things:
    –   housework (cleaning, ironing etc.)?
    –   meals (cooking them, eating them, clearing up after them)?
    –   travelling?
b   What do you *waste* time or money on?
c   When you have to *save* money, what do you save it on?

Point two

Problems, difficulties and *trouble* (N.B. *problems* and *difficulties* are **countable**, but *trouble* is usually **uncountable**) often have the same kind of construction with *-ing*, so we have put them in here. Here are some examples:

You'll have some difficulty opening a bank account here.

It's a problem getting hold of him in the afternoon.

It's no trouble cooking for three instead of two.

To practise this construction, complete these sentences – with true information if possible – and find someone to read them to.

a   At school I had problems _____ .

b   I have no difficulty _____ .

c   For me it's not a problem _____ .

d   I had some trouble _____ on my last holiday.

e   As regards money, I have difficulty _____ .

f   _____ doing this course.

Prepositions

Sometimes you don't know if a preposition is necessary, and sometimes you don't know the right preposition. So in these preposition exercises you have to decide two things:
    –   is a preposition needed?
    –   if so, what is the preposition?

There is always a gap, but sometimes you don't need to fill it.

We recommend you do this exercise in pencil.

a   One reason _____ going to England is to learn English.

b   He retired early because _____ his illness.

c   It all depends _____ you.

d   _____ the moment I can't afford to buy a car.

e   It's time we went _____ home.

f   Do you believe _____ ghosts?

g   I saw it _____ yesterday's newspaper.

h   You should contact the committee responsible _____ the plan.

i   Is my name _____ the list?

j   Put the address _____ the top of the page.

○━┳   *Rub out or white out the answers you got wrong. Leave it for a week, then redo the ones you didn't know.*

ADVICE   *If you are very strong-minded, you can write the problem sentences on separate cards, with the right answer on the back. Then play competitive games with the cards.*

Spelling

Days of the week and **months of the year** are particularly horrible to spell but they must be learnt.

a   Test yourself by writing down the days of the week and the months of the year from memory in two columns.

b   Then check them *letter by letter* in the Key – or get someone else to check what you have written.

c   Find which ones you get wrong. These are your personal spelling problems.

○━┳   Write them here (correctly):

_____

_____

ADVICE   *Decide how to learn these problem spellings. For example:*
  –   ask someone to dictate them to you next week
  –   write them on your bathroom mirror in soap
  –   visualize them and write them down three times in the next three days
  –   make a habit of writing the date in full in English, on everything you write each day.

PRESENTATION

Writing Tutorial

The 'good guy' and the 'bad guy'

Let's start with what your work looks like – that is, with *presentation* and *layout*.
Presentation is the general look and appearance of the work. *Layout* is the visible shape, the disposition of the parts on the page.

TASK 1

On the next two pages are two versions of the same composition.

The Bad Guy

Version A is obviously the 'bad guy'. But what exactly is wrong with it? Make a few notes below. Concentrate entirely on presentation and layout: ignore questions of spelling, punctuation and grammar. Use your dictionary to find the words you need. What is wrong with version A?

_____

_____

The Good Guy

Version B is equally obviously the 'good guy'. How? What is right with version B?

_____

_____

Version A

> In the Italian language we have many American words, for instance, when we say 'FAST FOOD' we mean "a place where we can eat a sandwich in a fast way. But "fast food" is a typical american word, others examples can be "spon sor" and "look", in the meaning of appearance for what concern the TV televisian programmes and the commercials on TV television, we can say that most of

Version B

June 1993

The Cultural Influence of the U.S.A.

In the Italian language we have many American words. For instance, when we say "fast food" we mean a place where we can eat a sandwich in a fast way – but "fast food" is a typical American expression. Other examples could be "sponsor" and "look", in the meaning of "appearance".

As regards television programmes and

So what are the differences? The big difference is that:
- Version A is a **first draft**
- Version B is a **final draft**.

First draft

The first draft of a piece of writing is for your eyes only. You can write it on anything – a piece of newspaper, a box of cigarettes, the wall. You can change it as much as you want. You can make silly mistakes which you correct later.

You can *cross things out*

~~Why does she go on so?~~

You can use *arrows* and *insertion marks*

quite

She usually (is) not so chatty.

You can use *asterisks** (like this one) and *footnotes*, *abbreviations* and *short forms*. You can write *sideways* or *upside down* or *in circles*

When I had finished writing this, I realised that I wanted to go back and start again. to the beginning of

You can do what you like. It is *not* for anyone else.

Final draft

The final draft is for showing to the public. It may be the second, third, fourth or fortieth draft. It will be very nearly perfect, and it will follow normal *document presentation requirements* for any document which is to be read by others:

1   Standard-size paper

Standard-size paper is called A4. This is the size of a piece of standard photocopy paper. It should be white.

2   Double-spaced writing

This means writing on every second line. It makes the writing easier to read and leaves space for the reader to write comments and corrections. Almost all articles for publication are presented double-spaced.

3   Easy to read

'Easy to read' means typed or very clearly written, with of course no crossing out, changes or insertions. Apart from looking bad, these really make the writing difficult to read.

If your handwriting is really awful, do something about it. This can be particularly important in exams: there is evidence that examiners are unconsciously influenced by bad handwriting and give lower marks.

ADVICE   **Learn to type.** *Typing is an essential skill these days and doesn't take long to learn.*

Get access to a word processor *and learn to use it. This is essential in any case for your future employment prospects.*

4   A margin

A margin makes the writing look good and gives the reader space to write comments. There are certain conventions about margins in English. They should be two to three centimetres wide, not half a centimetre and not half as wide as the page. And they should *always* be *on the left*.

5   A title

A title is essential for quick identification of the document.

6   A date

A date is essential, especially when there is a sequence of documents. Always date any documents you may produce. In this course both you and your tutor or teacher will need to know when each composition was written.

7   Proofreading

The document must have been checked for accuracy. When this is done before publication, it is called *proofreading* and we will call it this here. Proofreading is essential.

This does not mean that there will be no mistakes. One of the purposes of writing is to make mistakes and have them corrected. What it means is that there will be no mistakes which you yourself could have corrected.

In first drafts there are always mistakes. You forget a full stop, you miss an *s*, you misspell a word, you leave out a capital letter. These are simple things, things you know, things you yourself can see are wrong – *provided you check*.

No professional writer would let a document go to the public without a double check – at least two proofreadings. The same applies to you. Writing is your business. You too need to proofread – twice.

These are the normal *document presentation requirements*. All the work you present should fulfil them.

ADVICE   **Treat your work with respect.** *Make it look good before you send it into the world.* **Treat your reader with respect.** *Never hand over a first draft. Apart from being rude, it's counter-productive. Your reader won't enjoy reading it.*

TASK
2

This is a reinforcement exercise, just to help you remember. It is also good for your grammar. Below are the elements of the requirements we have been talking about. Write them out as a neat list of rules, in full sentences, but as briefly as possible.

date	typed	title	left-hand
A4 paper	margin	proofread	twice
clearly written	double-spaced	2 – 3 cms wide	

Example   a   *There should be a title.*

b   _____

c   _____

d   _____

e   _____

f   _____

g   _____

Reading

At this point in the Writing Tutorial you will have a choice. You can do the reading text at the end of the unit, or you can go straight on to the assignment. Before deciding, read about the text below.

Money

We start with a subject which is close to the heart – money. Money is symbolic. People love it, hate it, show off with it, tell lies about it, light cigars with it. It is a focus for irrational feelings and behaviour. That's what makes it interesting.

The reading text (pages 24–25) is a questionnaire surrounded with sayings. Use them to diagnose how *money-conscious* you are.

Start with the questionnaire. Compare your answers in a small group if possible. Circle the numbers to which your answer is yes.

Then read the sayings. Select the four or five sayings which best reflect your own personal attitudes, and circle their letters. Find out what others have selected and why.

Record your answers in the Key and decide if you agree with the interpretation (you should always be sceptical of questionnaires!).

ASSIGNMENT 1

MONEY

If you are a student, you probably don't have much money.

- What do you spend it on?

  What takes most of your money?

  How do you budget?

  What temptations do you have to resist?

  Do you have any arguments about money?

- Are you basically a gambler, a saver or a spender?

  . Does money occupy your thoughts a lot or do you seldom think about it?

- Would you like more money? But what do you want it for ?

  What are your (realistic) material goals?

! *Planning: making notes*

Before you start writing your first draft, write a few notes about your ideas. This is important. You need to get into the habit of *making notes*. *Notes*, not sentences – just a word or two for each thought that comes into your head, enough to help you remember the idea. To keep your notes about money short, write them in the box above, as in this example. You do not have to answer all the questions.

MONEY

If you are a student, you probably don't have much money. ← *Almost zero.*

- What do you spend it on? ← *Food, rent, nothing on clothes. Books a terrible price*

  What takes most of your money?

  How do you budget?   *No money, no temptations. But sometimes cassettes and cigarettes.*

  What temptations do you have to resist?

  Do you have any arguments about money?   *A saver–definitely–very old-fashioned–don't like banks– want money to be physical– would like to keep it in a*

- Are you basically a gambler, a saver or a spender?   *bag under the bed.*

  Does money occupy your thoughts a lot or do you <u>seldom think</u>
  about it?

  Hate thinking about it.

- Would you like more money? But what do you want it for ?

  What are your (realistic) <u>material goals</u>? ← *Not to have to think about money !*

FEEDBACK

To the reader

Please check that the writer has fulfilled all the document presentation requirements. Then react to the content: ask questions, comment, agree, etc. by writing a comment in the comment box. Don't make negative criticisms: just show your interest.

	YES/NO
The composition is on A4 paper.	
It is double-spaced.	
It is easy to read and has no changes, crossing out etc.	
It has a 2–3 cm. left-hand margin.	
It has a title.	
It has a date.	
It has been thoroughly proofread.	

Comment on content.

HOW MONEY-CONSCIOUS ARE YOU ?

a   Money is flat, and wants to be piled up.
Proverb

b   Neither a borrower nor a lender be.
Shakespeare 1564–1616

c   The greatest of evils
and the worst of crimes
is poverty.
G. B. Shaw 1856–1950

d   Easy come, Easy go.
Proverb

e   Money is round and
wants to roll.
Proverb

f   Getting and spending
we lay waste our life.
Wordsworth 1770–1850

g   I'm going to spend,
spend, spend!
Pools winner

h   How pleasant it is to have
money, heigh-ho!
How pleasant it is to have
money.
Arthur Hugh Clough 1819–61

i   What we gave, we have;
What we spent, we had;
What we kept, we lost.
(Epitaph)

j   Quarterly, is it, money reproaches me:
  'Why do you let me lie here wastefully?
I am all you never had of goods and sex,
  You could get them still by writing
a few cheques.'
Philip Larkin 1922–85

k   If you want to know what God
thinks of money, look at some
of the people he gives it to.
G. K. Chesterton 1874–1936

QUESTIONNAIRE

**Circle the *Yes* answers below. Then read the
sayings. Select four or five sayings which best
reflect your own personal attitudes, and circle
their letters.**

1   Do you dislike thinking about money?
2   Do you know the current prices of petrol,
milk, postage stamps?
3   Do you occasionally splash out on a big
celebration, no expense spared?
4   Are you interested in how much people earn?
5   Do you enjoy bargaining?
6   Do you usually shop around, i.e. compare
several prices before you buy?
7   Do you quite often buy things on impulse?
8   If you were selling a second-hand car, would
you describe its strong points enthusiastically?
9   Do you take home the still-packaged remains
of in-flight meals?
10   Do you pay bills at the last moment, so as to
get the extra interest on your money?
11   Do you usually remember if you owe someone
a drink or if they owe you one?
12   Do you sometimes spend more if you are using
a credit card?
13   Do you always know how much you have in
your bank, your purse and your pocket?

l   Credit is the lifeblood of
modern capitalism.
Susan George 1950-

m   Time is money.
Benjamin Franklin 1706–90

n There are few ways in which a man can be more innocently employed than in getting money.

Samuel Johnson 1709–84

o Money is a terrible master but an excellent servant.

Proverb

r For I don't care too much for money For money can't buy me love.

John Lennon 1940–80
Paul McCartney 1942–

s Money couldn't buy friends but you got a better class of enemy.

Spike Milligan 1918–

14 Would you normally go to some trouble to get a refund on an unused train ticket?
15 Do you sometimes forget when someone owes you money?
16 Does it disturb you if (now and then) you have nothing in the bank?
17 Do you claim all possible expenses against tax?
18 Do you say frequently 'I just don't know where it all went'?
19 Do you dislike most kinds of shopping?
20 Do you discuss best buys and other ways of saving money with friends?
21 Are you prepared to make a bet on a good prospect?
22 Do you check your bank statement carefully?
23 Do you add up bills in restaurants?
24 Would you be happy to buy your next TV on the instalment plan?
25 Do you like giving impromptu presents?
26 Do you give quite large sums to charity?

t Money makes the world go round.

The musical *Cabaret*

u It is easier for a camel to go through the eye of a needle, than it is for a rich man to enter the Kingdom of God.

The Bible

v When I die, I don't want to go to Heaven; I want to go shopping in America.

Julian Barnes 1946-

w Take care of the pence, and the pounds will take care of themselves.

Proverb

x Money is better than poverty, if only for financial reasons.

Woody Allen 1935–

y Money is like muck, not good except it be spread.

Francis Bacon 1561–1626

p To be clever enough to get a great deal of money, you must be stupid enough to want it.

G. K. Chesterton 1874-1936

q Money is power.

Proverb

z Annual income, twenty pounds, annual expenditure nineteen nineteen six, result happiness. Annual income twenty pounds, annual expenditure twenty pounds ought and six, result misery.

Charles Dickens 1812–70

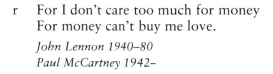

2 Language Preparation

! Look at Tests A and B for Unit 2, pages 149 and 152.

Narrative, the present perfect and the past

Do you know about the **present perfect** and the **past**? Here are some examples:

Present perfect	Past
*We **have never been** there.*	*We **were** there in April.*
*I **have enjoyed** your company.*	*I **enjoyed** your company.*
*He **has just robbed** a bank.*	*He **robbed** a bank.*

Many other languages have parallel verb forms. But in English their use is a little different. We want to draw your attention to just one aspect: you do not use the present perfect in telling stories; you use the **past tense**.

Stories, reports, history, anecdotes, any sequence of events in the past (that is, any **narrative**) – these are all in the **past tense**.

1 Practise recognizing where a narrative begins and ends. Here are three short friendly letters, each one with a small narrative in it somewhere. Find the *narratives* and underline them. ⌐━ㅠ

Dear Jo,

Have you finished your summer course? Will you get a bit of rest before starting work again? We love the toy you sent for Vera. She's a bit small to appreciate it now but I'm sure it will become one of her favourites. Rolf visited us for a week in July – he seemed very tired, but that didn't stop him from working: he dug the garden and planted lots and lots of vegetables. You can see we choose our friends carefully! We're off to Greece for a week to try to extend the summer – will give you a ring when we get back. Pat

---

Dear Liz,

Thinking of you – remembering this time last year! It's hard to believe a whole year has passed. I met Jackie on her way through from Hong Kong. She brought Jamie with her and we had a night out together – late, late, very late. I'm too old for that sort of thing. Anyway, she sends her love. And so do I.

Leslie

Dear Sol, We are using your cards to thank everyone for their presents so, of course, there's one for you too. We were sorry you couldn't come to the wedding, but I suppose Barcelona is a bit far. It all went very well, but really there were too many people: we were exhausted afterwards. We expect you in Spain sometime even if you don't like travelling.
Love, Nickie

2 In these two letters we have given you the choice of **past simple** or **present perfect** for some of the verbs. Identifying the **narrative** will help you to decide. Circle the appropriate tense.

> a   *I don't know what happened/has happened to Alex these last few days. You know we've always said how mean he is and how uninterested he is in helping with the house. Well, it seems that he reformed/has reformed. On Friday he offered/has offered to do the shopping, then yesterday he cleaned/has cleaned the bathroom and took/has taken the rubbish out without being asked – and while he was out he bought/has bought a cake for tea! We are all astonished and can't wait to see what happens next. The question is: why? We suspect that Irene has been talking to him.*

> b   *(From Australia) How are things with you? Many greetings from soggy Sydney. It's been/It was a little wet for me, but I hope it will improve. Luckily I haven't had/didn't have time to go to the beach anyway. I have left/left my driver's licence behind in England, but no problem - in half an hour I have had/I had a new one: and there has been/there was no queue, no delay. They have even smiled/even smiled at me! I might even say I have enjoyed/enjoyed the experience. I haven't seen/didn't see all the family yet - there are such a lot of them. I am working slowly down the list!*

ADVICE   *Read the texts aloud to get the feel for the use of the two tenses.*

Far, far away

There are some problems with using the word *far* – or rather, with *not* using it.

● *far* is *not* used for ordinary expressions of distance.

> *Liverpool is about 15 miles from Chester.* (*not* 'far from Chester')
> *The nearest petrol station is three kilometres away.* (*not* 'far away')

● When you really want to say something is *far*, you often use *a long way* instead of *far* (and sometimes *a long way away*). For example:

> *It's a long way away.*   X is *a long way* from Y.

● But you still use *far*:
  – with *too*   **It's too** *far to walk.*
  – for comparisons   *It's **further** than I thought.*
  – in questions   *How far is it?*

3 What would you say in these sentences? Read them aloud, preferably with a partner. Then write them.

a   I feel as if I'm _____ from home.

b   We've still got _____ to go.

c   New York is only three hours _____ by air.

d   Australia is much _____ than the USA.

e   Her house is just half a kilometre _____ mine.

f   Now you've really gone too _____ !

g   It's _____ to the station from here.

O—ᴍ   h   How _____ do you have to drive tonight?

Prepositions

4 Before you do this exercise, go back and revise the previous preposition exercise (page 16). As before, do the exercise in pencil – then, after checking it, rub out the prepositions you did not know so that you can revise them later. Don't forget – sometimes a preposition is not needed.

a   It's difficult to see a solution _____ this problem.

b   The exam committee is composed _____ three professors.

c   I'm planning to go _____ America this summer.

d   I get _____ home about six o'clock in the evening.

e   I read about it _____ *The Times* last week.

f   She told _____ her boss a long and unconvincing story.

g   We're going _____ holiday at the end of June.

h   The story is _____ page four.

i   It's _____ the bottom of the page.

j   This course will be finished _____ a month or two.

O—ᴍ   *Check in the Key, then rub out your errors.*

Punctuation: capital letters

You undoubtedly know what words have capitals in English:
- days of the week   – months of the year
- nationality adjectives (e.g. *French*, *English*)
- names of languages (e.g. *Italian*, *Swahili*)
- names of people and places   – the word 'I'

Make up a story including each of these categories.

2 YOUR VOICE

Writing Tutorial

Hot air

We want to introduce you to the concept of 'hot air'. Hot air is what is produced by someone who has nothing to say. Here is an example.

Terrorism is growing day by day...

Reader
> Is terrorism growing? I thought there was less of it.

Student
> Well, perhaps there is. I don't really know.

Reader
> So why did you say it was growing?

Student
> Oh, well, you know, something to say.

This writer felt that the composition expected him to say that terrorism was a problem – so that is what he said: hot air.

Another composition started like this:

> I think travelling is very good fun and interesting. When you travel you can meet many different nationalities and see their different habits and customs. You can also hear their languages and try to speak them yourself ...

The reader asked the writer about this composition. Their conversation went like this:

Reader	When did you last travel, Julie?
Julie	Last summer. We went to Spain.
Reader	Did you speak some Spanish?
Julie	No, we went all together in a group, so we spoke our own language.
Reader	But you had a good time?
Julie	Oh yes, except for the journey. There was an awful man who followed us around in the train.
Reader	Really? What did you do?
Julie	We had to lock ourselves in the lavatory for twenty minutes until he went away.
Reader	But you said in your composition that the reason you liked travelling was because you could meet foreigners and speak their language ...?
Julie	Oh, well, you know, something to say ...

Surprise

This conversation was a surprise both to the reader and to Julie.

Julie was surprised that she was expected to say something which was really true. Her idea was that if she wrote something very obvious the composition could be acceptable, even if there was no connection with her own reality.

The reader was surprised because she could not see any reason for writing such general things, especially since they were not true. This is not to say that they were lies – just that they had nothing to do with Julie's own experience. They were hot air. The reader felt that Julie should write to tell her something.

And Julie *did* have something to tell. The story of the man in the train was potentially very interesting. What did he look like? What did he say? Why did he choose to follow them and not someone else? What sort of person was he? *Why didn't she write about that?*

> THE MESSAGE   *Writing should have something to say.*

Even if your main motive is to pass an examination, don't waste your time writing about nothing. You will bore not only yourself but also your examiner.

TASK 1

Here are a few samples of writing. Which ones do you think sound like hot air and which ones seem to have something to say? Write your judgement next to each piece.

A

> *Violent crime is a terrible thing which should not be allowed. Nowadays violent crime is becoming more and more of a problem. Nobody knows what to do to solve this terrible problem.*

B

> *Many people think that punishment will not prevent crime, but I do not agree with them. In my town three years ago two men kidnapped and raped a 17-year-old girl and asked her family for a ransom . . .*

C

> *A vice that I deplore is jealousy, not only in a marriage but also in other aspects of life. For me, jealousy does not come from an absence of love but from an absence of trust in people. Perhaps jealous people have received little love from other people during their childhood.*

D

> *I wonder whether we will ever see an end to war. Every day there seem to be more people fighting in the world. I cannot understand how men can do these things. Will we ever have peace on earth and goodwill to all men?*

E

> *There are many different kinds of tree – big trees, small trees, evergreen trees, fruit trees and so on. Trees are very important in nature. They give shade in the summer and of course they provide wood for making furniture. Forests are also important …*

F

> *My sister smokes, and after lunch she always lights a cigarette, annoying the rest of the family. If there is one thing that gets on my nerves it is people who smoke at table …*

⊙━ᴘᴛ   *If you are not sure about which ones are hot air, check the Key.*

Having something to say

Writing can make your reader see things in a different way, give your reader new experiences. Everything you know or hear or see, everything that happens to you, is material to write about. Anything that strikes you can be used by you to strike your reader. Your daily life, your direct experiences, your thoughts and feelings, the TV, the newspaper, what people tell you – they are all transformed by you into what *you* have to say.

Look at the diagram to see how it works.

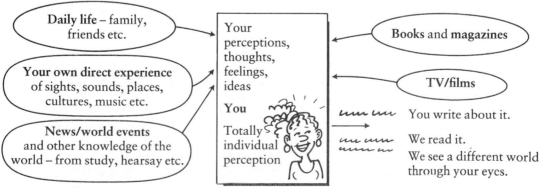

Courses and examinations

But, you say, 'producing words just to fill a piece of paper' – isn't that what we have to do in this course? What if we don't have anything to say on the subject? You have a very good point.

Triggers, bottle-openers, levers, launching pads

The subjects we give you in this course are meant to be triggers, bottle-openers, levers, launching pads: that is, ways of releasing what you want to say. They are meant to open doors in your mind, not shut them. If they don't open any doors for you, find something else to write about.

If, however, you are working for an examination, then you will need practice in writing to order, so stick to the given subjects. But don't let them dominate you. Make connections with what *you* want to say. Your readers want to hear it.

Cultivate your voice

One of the reasons why people find it difficult to say something in writing is simply that they have not said it in writing before. They are used to saying things face to face to people they know. They are *not* used to saying things in writing to people they don't know – so nothing comes when they try to write.

You need practice. So what you need is to cultivate your voice in writing: to get the habit of putting your experience, perceptions, ideas, reactions and interests on paper. Put your life in writing.

A writer's diary

For this purpose we suggest you keep a writer's diary. It will be a bit different from a normal diary. First, it will *not* record boring events. For example:

> **Tues. 16 October**
>
> Maria's birthday party. She's 23. I took the bicycle to Peter; he says it will need a new wheel. Lamb for dinner.

This is not what most people want to read. It is deeply boring. Instead, give us interesting observations – of people, for example.

> **Wed. 9 July**
>
> My brother Mick is obsessed with reading newspapers. It's strange because he doesn't read anything else (e.g. comics, novels) and also because he never talks about what he reads, though he must be very well-informed. He spends about two or three hours a day reading the paper.

Write for an outsider to read, and give all the necessary explanations.

> *November 3*
>
> *We were discussing which player we liked best in the football team. Anna,
> my sister, was keen on Thomas (he's the most famous player) because
> he's usually the one who scores the goals. But I said I liked Manfred best
> (he's the goalie). He's better-looking, for one thing, but that's not really
> the reason. He makes me feel secure whenever he saves a goal. I feel he's a
> good protector.*

Your diary entries can be short or long, as you wish, but they must have a good
range, i.e. they should deal with a lot of different subjects and draw inspiration
from a number of sources. For example, think about the world news:

> *. . . Today there has been a huge earthquake in Iran. Four hundred thousand
> dead, they say. It's hard to imagine.*

or your own feelings:

> *. . . Sometimes I wonder if I will ever finish studying. I just seem to go on
> and on and the exams never stop. And what happens after that? It's
> so hard to get a job. Sometimes I get depressed just thinking about it.*

or life's annoyances:

> *. . . My father spent three hours in the queue at the post office today just
> to post his tax form. Luckily he was able to take time off from work so he
> didn't lose money, but it is still a ridiculous waste of time . . .*

How a diary can help

Many professional writers keep a diary of this kind. It can do a lot for you.

- It makes you find the words you need to talk about your own life.
- It makes you start to look for things that are worth writing about.
- It often brings your semi-conscious ideas and feelings to the surface and tells
  you things you didn't know you knew.
- It gets you into the habit of writing.
- It gives you a stock – a collection – of recorded experiences which you can
  use in your public writing.

How often?

We can't *make* you write a diary and we don't want to; we can only suggest that
it is a very good idea. If you can find the time, you should aim to write something
at least twice a week during the whole period of this course. (N.B. Don't write it
at the same time as the assignment.)

Prompts

To extend your range we give you a 'diary prompt' in each unit of this course. You can use it if you want, or neglect it if you have something more interesting to write about.

Corrections

It is valuable to write a diary even if no one else ever sees it, but obviously it will be useful if you can get the English corrected from time to time. Ask your teacher/tutor if s/he is prepared to do this; if not, find a native speaker, or use your reader. Whoever it is, don't make it hard for them: just give them a few pages at a time.

Reading

First day off

If you want to hear somebody who really speaks in her own voice, read the text by Margaret Powell at the end of this unit.

Margaret Powell was born into a poor family in England early in this century. She became a servant when she was quite young and worked for several rich families, then she learned to be a cook. She eventually married a milkman, had four children and became a full-time housewife.

When she was nearly sixty she decided it was time she got an education – the education she missed when she was a child. So she went back to school. She studied history and English and she started to write the story of her life, of her experiences as a servant and as a cook.

Her books were instantly successful – probably because they sound so true (they *are* true) and because the writer's personality is so strong and clear. They sound as if she is speaking to you face to face.

In this episode, look at how the mood of the girl changes. It is interesting to find the point where the attention is mostly focused: is it a low point or a high point?

ASSIGNMENT 2

Do you remember one particular day in your life when you felt a strong sense of

● **expectation**
● **excitement**
● **liberation**  (освобождении)
● **anxiety**
● **disappointment**

Describe what happened and what you thought and felt.

Planning: getting ideas

● Make a few notes (not sentences).
● There is probably one particular moment of the day you remember best: what exactly do you remember? Note the physical details – what you felt/saw/heard. (You may exaggerate, but do not invent. Truth is much stranger, and more interesting, than fiction.)
● Think backwards from that moment – what led up to it?
● If you have a listener, tell him/her the story – in any language. See what questions and comments you get. Or record it on tape and see if it sounds interesting.
● When you write, put yourself back in the story and show it as it seemed at the time and in the order it happened.
● Check it for linguistic accuracy before you make your final draft. Make sure you have followed all the document presentation requirements.
● Give it to your reader.

FEEDBACK

To the reader

Please complete the questionnaire below. Check the layout and make sure it conforms to the document presentation requirements. Then write a comment about the *feelings* conveyed by the writer. If possible, discuss your comment with the writer.

   If you notice any specific language errors, point them out to the writer. But don't correct them in the composition unless the writer asks you to.

Document presentation requirements	YES/NO
A4 paper	
Double spacing	
Fair copy (no corrections, etc.)	
Margin	
Title	
Date	
Careful proofreading	
Comment:	

DIARY PROMPT

Look around your house and find an object (an ornament, a picture, something at the bottom of your cupboard, etc.) that means something to you. Tell us about it.

First day off

I was three days in my first place in London before I had a chance to go out. I arrived there on a Wednesday and as a Wednesday was going to be my one day off in the week, obviously I didn't get it that week, so my first time out was on the Sunday. I was allowed from three o'clock till ten o'clock every Sunday, but that first day it took me so long to do the washing up that I didn't get away until four.

So there I was, all ready at four o'clock to go out and I was mad to go and see Hyde Park because it was a place I had read about with its soapbox orators and the guardsmen in their red coats walking around. I asked the cook what number bus to get on because I didn't want to look like some provincial hick that had just come up to London and didn't know anything. I was going to ask for Hyde Park, hand over the right money and look as if I knew it all.

I got on the bus that she told me and I went upstairs right to the front so that I could see everything. I sat there for a long time looking all round and very soon it struck me that the buildings were really the same kind that you could see anywhere. But of course because they were in London I thought, oh well, they must be marvellous.

No conductor took my fare. One came up several times but he never reached the front of the bus. I sat on and on, looking. I thought it seemed a long way but I had no idea where things were. Then I could see that we were in a very seedy neighbourhood: dirty little shops, a very slummy place – much more slummy than some of the places around my home.

Before I could do anything about it the conductor came up and said, 'This is the terminus.' So I said, 'I haven't seen Hyde Park yet.' And he said, 'No, you bloody well won't see it on this bus either. You're going in the wrong direction.' 'But this is the right number,' I said. 'Yes,' he said, 'this is the right number but you're going the wrong way. You got on on the wrong side of the road.' 'Well, why didn't you come up and get my fare – why didn't you tell me?' So he said, 'You try being a conductor on a bloody London bus, and see if you tell people who don't know where they're going where they should be going.'

I got off the bus very crestfallen and not knowing what to do at all. So he said to me, 'Where did you want to go?' I told him I wanted to go to Hyde Park and also that it was my first time in London. So he said, 'What are you going to do now, then?' He thought for a moment. 'I'll tell you what,' he said, 'we'll be going back in twenty minutes. We're going over to the café to have a cup of tea – why don't you come over with us?' Well, I'd gone to London to have an adventurous life so I thought, 'Well, here goes,' and walked over to the café with him and the bus driver.

Over the tea we got talking and this bus driver (his name was Jack) asked me why I wanted to go to Hyde Park. 'Well,' I said, 'when you live down in my town you read about Hyde Park. Surely it's one of the sights of London, isn't it?' 'Well,' he said, 'don't go into Hyde Park at night on your own, it's full of prostitutes.' 'Oh,' I said, 'is it?' And that didn't damp my ardour at all: I just thought it was marvellous and I wanted to have a good look at them.

'Yes,' said Jack. 'There they are, dressed up in all their best clothes.' 'Well, what do they look like?' I said. 'Oh, they dress up in muslins and things like that.' 'Oh,' I said, 'like Greek soldiers that wear those things like ballet skirts.' Then Jack said, 'Perhaps they look silly but I wouldn't want to get in a fight with them. My father was in Greece during the war and he was always telling us about the Greek soldiers, how strong they were.' Then Jack made a joke.

I didn't understand the joke but everybody laughed so I laughed too. After all he was paying for my cup of tea. And anyway, I wanted a free ride back and I got one. I went upstairs again, and Jack kept running up and talking to me and then he made a date to meet me on my next night off.

So there on my first time out in London after months and months without a boyfriend in my own home town I'd met one and made a date with him.

3 Language Preparation

! Look at Tests A and B for Unit 3, pages 149 and 152.

Each other

You have probably seen the words *each other* (or *one another*). Do you use them yourself?

Point one

Each other is sometimes necessary if the action is *reciprocal* or *mutual*.

Loving *each other* is quite different from loving *yourselves*.

1 To practise these, try retelling the (extremely simplified) story of Romeo and Juliet, using *themselves/himself/herself* or *each other*. You will find you are using *each other* too much, but don't worry about it yet.

Romeo and Juliet were born into two families which hated [1]_____

and were always fighting. They never spoke to [2]_____ .

Romeo and Juliet met [3]_____ at a ball at Juliet's house (Romeo

was not invited). They saw [4]_____ across the crowded room and

fell in love with [5]_____ instantly. It was irresistible: they couldn't

help [6]_____ . They managed to meet [7]_____ once

or twice and got married secretly.

They wanted to run away together but they were separated from

[8]_____ . Romeo, thinking Juliet was dead, killed [9]_____

and Juliet, when she realized Romeo was dead, killed [10]_____ too.

Their families blamed [11]_____ for this tragedy and were finally

reconciled with [12]_____ .

Point two

Having learnt to use *each other*, now unlearn it a little. The fact is that you only use *each other* when you cannot avoid it. It is only necessary grammatically when the verb *must* have an object.

> *We have known **each other** for years.* (*know* must have an object)
> *They looked at **each other**.* (*look at* must have an object)
> *They kissed **each other**.* OR *They kissed.* (*kiss* does not always need an object).

In the Romeo and Juliet story, where is *each other* really necessary? Take it away where you think it is not essential (and any words that go with it).

How well do you know them?

All languages have words for the various stages of acquaintance with other people, but the way the words are used is sometimes different.

In English the processes of meeting and getting to know people are distinct from the state of knowing them.

These people are **meeting**.
They may never **get to know** each other.

These people are probably
getting to know each other.
Some (often Americans) might
say they are **getting acquainted.**

These people have probably
known each other for a long time.

ADVICE   *The same is true for information. 'Knowing' something is a state, not an action. What you* do *is* **finding out, learning, discovering;** *the* result *is* **knowing.**

What would you use in these contexts?

a   In these last three years I have met a lot of people but _____ only a few of them.

b   It's not always easy to _____ new people in London.

c   At the airport I _____ a flight attendant who helped me.

d   I would like to _____ them better.

e   Rod has decided to come and visit you so that you can _____ him better.

f   During the trip we gradually _____ each other.

g   That's the disco where I _____ my first boyfriend.

h   How long have you _____ her?

i   We don't _____ anything about mushrooms: we'll have to _____ .

j   Who _____ what will happen in the future?

Prepositions

Before you start, revise the previous preposition exercise. Don't forget: sometimes a preposition may not be needed.

4

a Perhaps we do not need reasons _____ everything we do.

b From London, we'll travel _____ Scotland.

c Why don't you come _____ home, Bill Bailey?

d He didn't answer _____ my letter.

e The reason was that he was away _____ leave that week.

f All the information is _____ the brochure.

g *Spaghetti bolognese* consists _____ pasta with meat sauce.

h We were all _____ TV – did you see us?

i I would really like to participate _____ this programme.

j They asked _____ the kidnappers to let them go.

Check in the Key and rub out your errors.

5

Go back through the previous preposition exercises and find all the expressions which are concerned with *paper* (there are seven). Try to work out the principles involved (when do you use *in*, *at*, or *on*?).

Spelling: ie and ei

Here are four common words, each with two letters missing. Are the letters *ie* or *ei*?

rec__ __ve   p__ __ce   ch__ __f

If you are not sure, there is a rule about *ie* and *ei* (pronounced /iː/). It is
    'i before e except after c'.
It is not a universal rule but it applies to most cases, including the examples above. If you have a problem with this aspect of spelling, try applying this rule in the exercise below.

6

Decide whether these words are spelt with *ie* or *ei*.

a The *c__ __ling* was 3 metres high.

b He spoke very *br__ __fly*.

c This is a great *ach__ __vement*.

d Did you get a *rec__ __pt* when you bought the petrol?

e Do not *dec__ __ve* me.

f I was very *rel__ __ved* when I heard she was safe.

g I don't *bel__ __ve* you.

h Do you think I'm a *th__ __f*?

CRITERIA

Writing Tutorial

What comes next?

Presentation is important, but it doesn't have much to do with the quality of the content. Double-spacing, clear handwriting and good proofreading don't make the actual writing good.

Having something to say is vital, but it is not enough. What comes after that? What makes one piece of writing better than another – more readable, more interesting, more coherent, more memorable?

TASK 1

On the following pages you will find four compositions. They were all written in the same university English examination and they are all exactly as they were written, mistakes and all. Only the names have been changed. The subject was the same as your assignment in this unit, and the reading in the examination was based on the reading text in this unit.

Read the four compositions carefully – at least twice – and decide which you think is the best, which the second best and so on. Apply your objective judgement, but do not neglect your personal reactions (interest, boredom, enjoyment). Discuss the compositions with others if you are working together.

Then rank them from one to four and write your reasons in the table on page 44.

COMPOSITION A

I know a boy called Don that lives near me. He is 26 years old. He comes from a little town that is in the south: he lives in this city since he was seventeen.

I don't know very much about him and about his family, but I really think he hasn't ever got a true family.

He lives in a little pension and now he doesn't have a job. He's a very good boy: he's nice and kind with everybody. He has got many problems. First of all he cannot read or write because he doesn't even know what does it mean the word 'school'. He hasn't got any friends so he's very shy. Instead of all these things he has made all kinds of works to survive. For that I know he has never stolen anything: he likes to work, but he hasn't got many possibilities to do that. Everytime that I see him, I ask him how is it going and if he needs something.

He always answers that is all right and that he doesn't need anything. But I know that what he really needs is a family and so much love.

COMPOSITION B

I know a special person. This person is mister Hart, is a old man. He lives in a small home near the sea. I have been knowing him for two year because my parents bought a house near the sea two years ago. Mr Hart is in his sixties, he has a little dog, it is all white with a point black on the left eye. The name of the dog is Caesar. This dog is fantastic because it do a lot of things, like running on a ball. So Mr Hart takes his dog and goes towards the place of Logan, (this is a little town near the sea, on the south caost). When Mr Hart arrives at the place, he tracks the attencion of people, and the show beging. Caesar jumps up the ball and begins to run on it. All people are attonit for the little dog and for the old Mr Hart who sings a old song, (I sang that song when I was child with others children all around). So people give something to Mr Hart that in this way is making an honest living.

COMPOSITION C

My housemaid Tania is a very nice woman. She's forty-seven. I first met her two years ago when she came to substitute another housemaid who was pregnant.
At the beginning we were very embarassed but after meeting day, we became friends.
We have a beautiful relationship: we understand each other and try to solve any problem together. She usually comes at eight o'clock in the morning and remains till eleven.
Before working we drink a cup of coffee and talk about our plans for the day.
After coffee she begins cleaning the house which usually is in a big mess. She cleans the kitchen, the bedrooms, the bathrooms and finally the sitting-room. She's very good at doing her job, in fact all the rooms of the house smell good when she goes out.
As I was saying before we talk a lot and try to solve our problems together.
She's mainly preoccupied about her husband, money, and daughters.
In fact one of her daughters is going to get married in September and now, Tania has to prepare everything for the ceremony.
Sometimes we also talk about aesthetic problems: she isn't very slim and wants to loose weight, so she's following a very hard diet.
I like her because she has a lot of rare qualities: she's sincere, comprehensive, funny and honest.
I know she's precious and I would be very sad if she ever decided to go away.

COMPOSITION D

> Today everyone desires to have a professional job. That's a great problem.
> All our society is changing. We try to study to get a better social position.
> That's right, I'm sure. But on the contrary I need to study and to
> understand my life and life in general. I consider very iportant the school,
> that's the base of society, but at the same time I respect so much all
> people like the Babe*, to hope in a better future where and when we have no
> social difference. I know much people so attracted to their work but I think
> that's more easy: they are teachers, lawyers, doctors etc. The Babe's
> work is very difficult and heavy, but she's happy at the same, peraphs
> more than all the people that makes a professional work.
> The meaning of the Babe's consideration "I'm making an honest living,
> whoever looks down on me, they're lower than I am" is wonderful. In these
> lines I compered a friend of mine to Babe. She is a checker too, and I knew
> her when I came to live in Rome. I felt her immediately friendly. She enjoys
> very much to work as checker because she has the possibility to
> comunicate with different people, to stay with them and, sometimes, to
> help someone with a simple good word or a smile. It always seems she has
> no problem and I like all that.

*Babe is the character in the reading passage (at the end of this unit).

COMPOSITION	GOOD POINTS	WEAK POINTS	RANK 1 TO 4
A	_____	_____	
	_____	_____	_____
B	_____	_____	
	_____	_____	_____
C	_____	_____	
	_____	_____	_____
D	_____	_____	
	_____	_____	_____

Obviously there is no right answer to this exercise. Many of your comments will
be subjective and even the grading is not indisputable.

What the examiners say

Below is what the examiners said about these four compositions. See if you agree.

COMPOSITION A Touching story and shows promise. Some fairly important errors and the language is limited.   5/10   BORDERLINE

COMPOSITION B Nice story but the English is full of terrible mistakes and very basic.   4/10   FAIL

COMPOSITION C Reads easily but a bit wandering – could use better organization and desperately needs paragraphing. Good command of normal English.   7/10   GOOD

COMPOSITION D Ambitious content. Some oddities and not always clear, but some range of expression. Some rather basic errors. Takes a long time getting to the actual topic and the ending is a bit inconclusive.   6/10   PASS

Criteria

You will see that the examiners applied several different criteria when evaluating these compositions. If we take their comments apart, bit by bit, you will see some of these criteria emerging.

TASK 2

Here are the names of these criteria. Put them in the appropriate boxes.

accuracy   range   interest of content
clarity   form and relevance   fluency

	CRITERION
1 Touching story Nice story Ambitious	
2 The language is limited Good command of normal English Very basic Good range of expression	
3 Reads easily	
4 A bit wandering Could use better organization Desperately needs paragraphing Takes a long time getting to the actual point The ending is inconclusive	
5 Not always clear	
6 Some fairly important errors Full of terrible mistakes Some basic errors	

How have you classified the comments?

1   The first set of comments have to do with the *interest* of the content –
    imaginative, intellectual, perceptual.
2   The second group of comments is about the amount of language the writer
    has – the variety of vocabulary, the number of different kinds of sentence.
    We call this *range*.
3   The third comment is about *fluency*. Fluency is associated with *range*. It has
    to do with how natural the language sounds, how easily and quickly it comes.
4   The fourth set of comments concerns the structure of the writing, the balance
    and the coherence. We can put these together and call them *form*.
5   *Clarity* is the criterion here.
6   These last comments have to do with language *accuracy*, or correctness.

TASK
3

Now go back to the comments you made on the compositions at the beginning.
Which of these criteria did you apply? Which did you neglect?

From accuracy to interest

Your own strengths and weaknesses

The next question is how your own writing relates to these criteria. What are
your personal strengths and weaknesses?

You will need to get at least two judgements here: your own and your teacher/
tutor's. But before you do this, take a closer look at what each criterion involves.

When you have read about the criteria, you will be asked to evaluate your
own writing. So *as you read, think about how each one applies to you.*

Accuracy

It is not possible to make *no* errors when you are learning a language. But there
are different kinds of error, more or less important.

Proofreading mistakes   You yourself can correct these – for example, forgetting
a capital letter, or copying a name wrongly. These result from poor proofreading.

Basic errors   These reveal that you have not mastered some fundamental aspect of
English grammar. Here are some horrors:

Error	Correct
We don't can do it	→ We **can't** do it
The others students	→ The **other** students
a car beautiful	→ A beautiful car

If you are making mistakes like these regularly then you should really be
worrying.

Acceptable errors   These occur with things you are still learning or have not
even started to learn. For example, you might use *few* instead of *a few*, or
possibility instead of *opportunity*. Perhaps you don't know the difference
between a *president* and a *chairman* or you have trouble with a construction like
I'd never have had to .... Often ambitious writers make errors of this kind
because they are trying out new things. However, if you are making hundreds of
mistakes, then you may need to pay more attention to accuracy.

Range

One good way to see what range of language means is to look at what happens when it is missing. For example:

PETS

I don't like dogs, I like cats. I think cats are nicer than dogs. Dogs are not very nice. They jump on you. I don't like dogs. We have cats in our house. We haven't any dogs.

This is perfectly accurate – not a single mistake. So what is wrong with it?

From a purely linguistic point of view, it lacks *range*.

- It is really limited.
- There are only seven vocabulary items.
- There is only one tense.
- There are no conjunctions at all.
- Almost all the sentences are extremely simple.
- There is no variety of vocabulary, sentences and structures.

Range of language is a great virtue, but not the main one. Writing can have a wonderful range of language and still say nothing. The real virtue is *range of thought*, with a wide range of language to serve it.

Fluency

Fluency is something to do with range. We do not know what it is exactly but we recognize it when we see it. It is something that language learners often have when they have been exposed to the real language a lot, and something they do not usually have if they have learnt English only with a grammar book at school. The fluent writer produces a lot of expressions which are commonly used in everyday English; it sounds like the real language, not like a computer. Fluency is a great asset but again it is just hot air if it is not helping someone to say something.

Clarity

Lack of clarity is not a frequent problem at intermediate level. Some writers do not make their points sufficiently explicit, so that the reader feels lost. More seriously, a few writers mix basic errors with over-ambitious translations from their first language and produce completely incomprehensible language. If this is your problem you need to learn to write simple sentences in simple words.

Form

A composition should have a good shape.

- It should be to the point, that is, relevant. It shouldn't wander away on a different path and never come back.
- It should have a beginning, a middle and an end. Most writers have no problem with the beginning and the middle but sometimes don't know how to end. You are not alone. Even great writers have this difficulty.
- It should be well organized, i.e. it should be in parts, each part should be mainly about one thing and the parts should be in a logical order.
- The organization should be, to some extent, visible and explicit. This means:
  - paragraphs which reflect the parts
  - clear connections between the parts
  - words which tell you what the parts are about.

Some writers have a lot of trouble with form. It becomes increasingly important as your essays get longer and more complicated, and begin to move from direct experience to dealing with issues.

Interest

We have left interest to the last because it is the most important. In the end, interest is all that matters and all the other aspects of writing are only there to serve it. Interest means two things.

1   It means your personal interest in what you are saying. If you are bored, your reader will be bored too.
2   It means your ability to communicate your interest to your readers, so that they feel it too. That is what good writing is about.

If you feel you haven't anything to say, you will have to change your mind. Everyone has something to say: it is just a question of finding it.

If you have a lot of interesting things to say but your English is not yet up to saying them, you are lucky: you have only the easy things to learn!

Self-evaluation

Here is a table to help you evaluate your own writing. Before you get anyone else's opinion, *make up your own mind.* You are in some ways the best judge. You are the person who has most experience of yourself; you have had comments from past teachers; you know what gives you difficulties; you have seen other people's writing and can make comparisons. Mark what you think are your main strengths and weaknesses.

● Don't be excessively vain. You would not be doing this course if you did not have some room for improvement.
● Don't be excessively humble. Obviously everybody needs to improve in everything, but we are interested here in *relative* strengths and weaknesses. Give yourself credit for your good points.

Write 'strong' or 'weak' as appropriate.

	Your assessment	Teacher/tutor's assessment	Reader's assessment
ACCURACY			
RANGE AND FLUENCY			
CLARITY			
FORM			
INTEREST			

Teacher/tutor's evaluation

When you have done this, arrange to get your teacher/tutor's opinion. S/he has by now marked three of your compositions and should be able to form a tentative judgement.

Make an appointment if possible. Take your past compositions to the appointment so that your teacher can look at them again. If an appointment is not possible, hand in the table (with or without your own assessment) and your previous compositions and ask for an evaluation in terms of the criteria.

Reader's evaluation – feedback

The reader of your assignment in this unit is asked to pick out the strong points. You may like to see how his/her reaction compares with the other evaluations.

Priorities

Finally, what are your priorities? Where do you want to concentrate your efforts? This depends on you and your situation.

- **Your personal purposes in practising writing.** If, for example, you are using writing to improve your English generally, you may be most interested in increasing your range.

- **Your personal strengths and weaknesses.** If you know that you are particularly bad at organizing your thoughts, or communicating your interest, you may want to put these first.

- **External constraints such as examinations.** If you are aiming at an examination, you *must* try to find out the examination criteria. In some exams, for example, accuracy is everything. Try to get a description of the exam; if there is none, you can sometimes guess the criteria from instructions in old exam papers, from other people's results or just from the personality of the examiners.

So what are your personal priorities?

1 _____

2 _____

Reading

Babe Secoli

This reading text is the one which helped to inspire the four compositions at the beginning of this unit. It comes from a fascinating book called *Working* by an American journalist, Studs Terkel. He interviewed hundreds of Americans about their work: rich and poor, professional and non-professional, publishers and prostitutes. Then he transcribed and edited the interviews and published them.

The book shows a tremendous range of attitudes to work, from disgust and boredom through interest to obsession. One of the most interesting aspects is the effort so many people make to find value and pride in their jobs.

Look at Babe Secoli's attitude to the various aspects of her work – and consider if you would feel the same. Also decide how you feel about her and what kind of personality emerges from her words. What do you think are her most characteristic words?

N.B.   Babe Secoli is not an educated woman, and some of her speech is non-standard.

ASSIGNMENT 3

Think of a person you know, perhaps from your area or town, someone who doesn't have a professional job.

Describe this person

- **How do you know him/her?**
- **What does s/he do?**
- **What problems does s/he have?**
- **How does s/he feel about life in general?**

Planning: notes

Keep writing *notes* – not full sentences and not in lines. Write them on the assignment page, anywhere you like.

There is a reason for asking you to write notes. Organizing a composition involves *selecting* the most interesting of your ideas and *re-arranging* them for maximum coherence and impact. It is difficult to do this if you have already started putting your ideas in line, one after the other. It is also difficult to do this with full sentences – partly because full sentences are too long to move around.

So put down everything you can think of in notes – freely. Use the white space on the page. Also put down some characteristic things that the person you have thought of does or says.

ADVICE   *When you are ready to start writing, look at your notes and decide what you are going to say at the end of the composition. A good principle is to keep the best to the last. Then start your first draft.*

FEEDBACK

To the reader

Please complete the questionnaire below.

1   Have all the document presentation requirements been fulfilled? Please tick (✓).

A4 paper	Double spacing
Fair copy	Margin
Title	Date
Proofreading	

2   What do you think is/are the *strong and the weak points* of this composition? Write *strong* or *weak* as appropriate. You do not have to fill all the boxes.

Accuracy	Range/Fluency	Clarity	Form	Interest

3   Say briefly what you think of the person the writer has described.

_____

_____

DIARY PROMPT

The animals in your life (from insects to elephants). What are your thoughts and feelings? Love? Indifference? Revulsion? Respect? Anxiety? Concern? Are you different from other people in your responses? What incidents with animals stick in your mind? Why?

BABE SECOLI

She's a checker at a supermarket. She's been at it for almost thirty years.

I started at twelve – a little, privately owned grocery store across the street from the house. They didn't have no cash registers. I used to mark the prices down on a paper bag.

When I got out of high school, I didn't want no secretary job. I wanted the grocery job. It was so interesting for a young girl. I just fell into it. I don't know no other work but this. This is my life.

We sell everything here, millions of items. From potato chips and pop – we even have a genuine pearl in a can of oysters. It sells for two something. Snails with the shells on, fanciness. There are items I never heard of we have here. I know the price of every one. Sometimes the boss asks me and I get a kick out of it. There isn't a thing you don't want that isn't in this store.

You sort of memorize the prices. It just comes to you. I know half a gallon of milk is sixty-four cents; a gallon, one dollar ten cents. You look at the labels. A small can of peas, Raggedy Ann, Green Giant, that's a few pennies more. I know Green Giant's eighteen and I know Raggedy Ann is fourteen. I know Del Monte is twenty-two. But lately the prices jack up from one day to another. Margarine two days ago was forty-three cents. Today it's forty-nine cents. You just memorize. On the register is a list of some prices, that's for the part-time girls. I never look at it.

I don't have to look at the keys on my register. I'm like the secretary that knows her typewriter. The touch. My hand fits. The number nine is my big middle finger. The thumb is number one, two and three up. The side of my hand uses the bar for the total and all that.

I'm eight hours a day on my feet. It's just a physical tire of standing up. When I get home I get my second wind. As far as standing there, I'm not tired. It's when I'm roaming around trying to catch a shoplifter. There's a lot of shoplifters in here. When I see one, I'm ready to run for them.

When my boss asks me how I know, I just know by the movement of their hands. And with their purses and their shopping bags and their clothing re-arranged. You can just tell what they're doing and I'm never wrong so far.

The best kind shoplift. They're not doing this because they need the money. A very nice class of people off Lake Shore Drive. They do it every day – men and women. Lately it's been more or less these hippies, living from day to day . . .

It's meats. Some of these women have big purses. I caught one here last week. She had two big packages of sirloin strips in her purse. That amounted to ten dollars. When she came to the register, I very politely said 'Would you like to pay for anything else, without me embarrassing you?' My boss is standing right there. I called him over. She looked at me sort of on the cocky side. I said 'I know you have meat in your purse. Before your neighbours see you, you either pay for it or take it out.' She got very snippy. That's where my boss stepped in. 'Why'd you take the meat?' She paid for it.

Nobody knows it. I talk very politely. My boss doesn't do anything drastic. If they get rowdy, he'll raise his voice to embarrass them. He tells them not to come back in the store again.

I have one coming in here, it's razor blades. He's a very nice dressed man in his early sixties. He doesn't need these razor blades any more than the man in the moon. I've been following him and he knows it. So he's laying low on the razor blades. It's little petty things like this. They're mad at somebody, so they have to take their anger out on something.

We had one lady, she pleaded with us she wanted to come back – not to have her husband find out. My boss told her she was going to be watched wherever she went. But that was just to put a little fright in her. Because she was just an elderly person. I would be too embarrassed to come into a store if this would happen. But I guess it's just the normal thing for these days – any place you go. You have to feel sorry for people like this. I like them all.

My family gets the biggest kick out of the shoplifters: 'What happened today?' (Laughs) This is about the one with the meat in her purse. She didn't need that meat any more than the man in the moon.

Some of them, they get angry and perturbed at the prices, and they start swearing at me. I just look at them. You have to consider the source. I just don't answer them, because before you know it I'll get in a heated argument. The customer's always right. Doesn't she realize I have to buy the same food? I go shopping and pay the same prices. I'm not getting a discount. The shoplifters, they say to me 'Don't you want for something?' Yes, I want, and I'm standing on my feet all day and I got varicose veins. But I don't walk out of here with a purse full of meat. When I want a piece of steak I buy a piece of steak.

My feet, they hurt at times, very much so. When I was eighteen years old I put the bathing suit on and I could see the map on my leg. From standing, standing. And not the proper shoes. So I wear like nurse's shoes with good inner sole arch support, like Dr Scholl's. They ease the pain and that's it. Sometimes I go to bed, I'm so tired that I can't sleep. My feet hurt as if I'm standing while I'm in bed.

I'm a checker and I'm very proud of it. There's some, they say, 'A checker – ugh!' To me, it's like somebody being a teacher or a lawyer. I'm not ashamed that I wear a uniform and nurse's shoes and that I got varicose veins. I'm making an honest living. Whoever looks down on me, they're lower than I am.

4 Language Preparation

! Look at Tests A and B for Unit 4, pages 150 and 152.

Zero article

A special feature of English is that nouns which have a *general sense* have no definite article – no *the*. The presence of *the* is very significant in English. For example, if you say 'Butter's too fattening' we will understand that you mean butter *in general*. If you say '*The* butter's too fattening' we will assume that you are talking about some *specific* butter.

This means that many students of English have to learn to stop saying *the* when they are speaking generally.

1 To get the feeling of generalizing without *the*, write something true, or interesting, or both, but always *general*, about these:

a Young men with motorbikes _____ .

b _____ school-leaving exams.

c _____ cats and dogs _____ .

d Happiness _____ .

e _____ modern rock music.

f _____ football on TV _____ .

g Cosmetics _____ .

h _____ prices _____ .

i _____ new furniture _____ .

j Carrots _____ .

! *Get your sentences checked by an expert.*

2 Below are some sentences written by learners of English. Some *the*s are correct; some are wrong. Take out the ones you feel are wrong.

a The Constitution of the United States was written with the free trade principles in mind.

b Capitalism gives priority to the material things such as the cars, the houses, the clothes.

c The economic growth in America at that time resulted in a reduction in the inflation and the unemployment.

d He discovered in himself a great love for the nature and the animals.

Enabling

Often one event makes it possible for another one to happen. We want to look at four ways of saying this. Here is a mini-story.

On Sunday the weather was good, so we began to learn deep-sea diving. We could all swim, we were all in good health and we all had a lot of experience of skin-diving.

Put it another way:

The good weather _____	allowed us to	
Experience with skin-diving _____	helped us to _____	learn deep sea diving.
Good health _____	enabled us to	
Being able to swim _____	made it possible (for us) to	

Allow, *help*, *enable* and *make it possible* can often be used interchangeably, one instead of the other. But you can see that sometimes there is a little difference between them.

- If X *enables* you to do something, it means that without X you could not do it – X *makes it possible*.
- If X *helps* you to do it, then without X it would be more difficult (but not impossible).
- If X *allows* you to do something, it provides the right conditions – but you don't necessarily do it.

! With these expressions you must say *who* is helped, enabled etc.

*This will enable **them** to . . .*   *This will help **our group** to . . .*
*This will allow **the government** to . . .*

The exception is *make it possible to*, which is the only one which can be used impersonally.

Fill the spaces in the sentences with a suitable verb (use a variety) and get the construction right. The first one is done for you as an example.

a   The TV _____*helps people to*_____ keep up-to-date.

b   Bank loans _____ buy houses.

c   This law _____ import more cars.

d   Shop sales _____ get rid of old stock.

e   Studying others _____ understand ourselves.

f   Cars _____ get about faster.

g   An outside stairway _____ escape from the building in case of fire.

! *There are no right answers to this exercise, but you should check it with a friend or a teacher.*

Prepositions

Revise previous errors, and go on working in pencil.

a   There is a great demand _____ more and more soap operas.

b   This course is made up _____ several components.

c   Who starred _____ the classic film *Gone with the Wind*?

d   We were supposed to meet under the clock _____ ten.

e   He's flying _____ Finland on Friday.

f   Sometimes they don't answer _____ the telephone at all.

g   I'm expecting a reply _____ the next few months.

h   It depends mainly _____ who wins the election.

i   _____ that time I was still in love with Fiona.

j   I was taking part _____ group therapy sessions to please her.

 Check in the Key and erase errors.

Look through the previous preposition exercises, and find:
- all the expressions that have to do with *travel* (there are three – holidays and going home don't count);
- all the prepositions that have to do with *parts, elements, the composition of things* (there are three).

What is the characteristic preposition in each case?

 Check in the Key if you are not sure.

Punctuation

What is the difference between the A sentences and the B sentences below? Which look right to you? Decide what you think before going on.

A We believe, that all men are created equal.	**B** We believe that all men are created equal.
It is not true, that writing is difficult.	It is not true that writing is difficult.
They said, no.	They said no.
I want to know, why you're here.	I want to know why you're here.

In fact the B sentences are punctuated correctly. In English you don't normally put a comma (,) before what is *thought, believed, said* – unless there is an extra phrase in that position which needs commas. For example:

   We believe, *as a matter of principle*, that all men are created equal.

Look through these sentences carefully and put in additional commas where you think they are really necessary.

a   I would suggest that Christmas be moved to July.

b   Since they believe the world is flat, they also think it's possible to fall off.

c   He thinks he is sick and he says he is sick, but I have the feeling on the whole that he is perfectly all right.

d   There is no doubt that animals affect people in many ways. It is clear for example that having a pet often improves people's health.

4 USING FEEDBACK

Writing Tutorial

> **feedback** /'fiːdbæk/ *noun* [U] information about sth that you have done or made which tells you how good or successful it is: *We need some more feedback from the people who use our textbooks.*

Oxford Wordpower Dictionary

> *Feedback* is a response or reaction from another person to something you do, that can be used to help you assess and improve on your performance in the future.

Think of the times in your life when you have used or needed feedback, maybe for a project, piece of research, new idea etc.

Let's take an example:

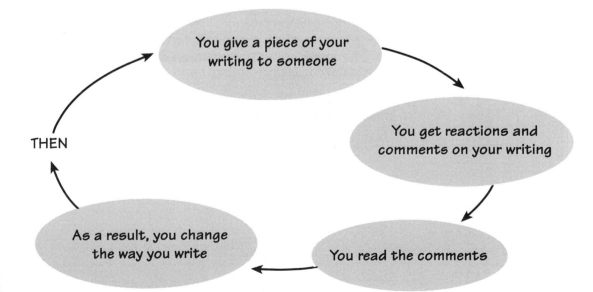

The feedback loop

This is the *feedback loop*. You do something, you get feedback, you do it again but differently, you get more feedback, and so on. The feedback is the comments and reactions of your reader(s) and your teacher/tutor. They come back to you and they feed you.

This is one of the ways learning happens. To improve your writing you need feedback. But to make feedback work, you need two conditions:

1   the feedback must be useful and usable
2   you must use it.

If your reader's or your teacher's comments are no use, or if you don't read them, or if you read them and forget them immediately, then there is no feedback.

This part of the course is about getting the right kind of usable feedback from your teacher and using the feedback you get.

Forms of feedback

Detailed feedback on written work usually comes to you in three forms:

1   the teacher's 'marking' or correction of your writing
2   comments on your writing from your teacher or reader
3   the mark or grade you get for your writing (if any).

What do teachers do?

Teachers have different responses to written work, as you undoubtedly know.

Marking

Sometimes they correct everything. Sometimes they just underline errors and don't correct them. Sometimes they tell you the kind of error but they don't correct it. Sometimes they do all three.

Comments

Some write nothing; some write 'Good', 'Better', 'Terrible'; some put ticks (✓) which mean OK, good; some write detailed comments and advice, e.g. 'Do some work on indirect questions' or 'Needs paragraphing'. Some comment only on accuracy, some mainly on content, and so on.

Grades

Some don't give a grade, some indicate whether the composition would pass the examination, some give a number (e.g. 6/10) and some give A, B, C, D, etc. In this case you need to know what the numbers or letters mean.

Colours

Some teachers do everything in red ink. Some use a pencil. Some use a black or blue pen. This can make a difference to the way you use feedback, and also to the way you feel about it.

What does your teacher do at the moment?

Marking _____

Comments _____

Grades/Marks _____

Pen/Pencil _____

What do you do?

You need to decide what forms of teacher feedback will be most useful to you. This will depend on what you do with the feedback. As we said before, the feedback must be *useful* and *usable*, but it must also be *used*.

TASK 1

On the next two pages are some ways of using marking feedback. Read them through and indicate:
  – what you do at the moment
  – what you would like to try in future.

Choose just *one* approach for the future. Use your common sense. As you will see, some of the approaches take more time or mental effort than others. Decide which you prefer on the basis of your knowledge of your own character. Obviously you want the most results with the least effort – but you do want results!

   Your decision is not binding. Nobody is going to make you use one approach or another. You can experiment as much as you want. But you must do *something*.

   Write what you do at the moment:

_____

Decision

When you have decided how you want to use feedback, write your decision below. Choose *one* option only.

_____

Ways of using feedback

A MEMORIZING

Your work is corrected. You check that you understand the corrections, then you try to memorize the correct versions. You keep the corrected writing and look at it from time to time.

B RE-WRITING I

You make a photocopy of your work before you hand it in. When you get the corrected work back you check that you understand the corrections. Then you blank out the incorrect version on the photocopy and write in the correct one. You now have a much improved composition. You read through all your 'improved' compositions from time to time.

C RE-WRITING II (for those with word processors)

When you get your corrected work, you check that you understand the corrections. Then you amend the document in the word processor and print out an improved version of your composition. You read this through from time to time.

D SELF-CORRECTION

You photocopy your composition before you hand it in. When you get the work back you study the mistakes and check that you understand them. A week later you try to correct the photocopy of the original version. You check your corrections with the corrected version.

E COLLECTING POINTS

Your work is corrected and you check that you understand the corrections. Then you make notes on the points to remember, e.g.
  'depend *on* (not *of*)'
  'Can't use *use to* in the present – only *used to* in the past'
You write your notes very clearly, as messages to yourself. You re-read your messages regularly.

F INDUCTION I

You ask to have your mistakes not corrected but marked with a code to show what kind of mistake it is, e.g. GR = Grammar, V = Vocabulary, P = Punctuation. When you get your work back, you try to work out what the mistakes are and to correct them. When you next see your teacher you check that you were right.

This approach works best if the teacher corrects *some* mistakes and codes only the ones you are able to work out for yourself.

N.B. It is *essential* to check that your corrections are right.

G INDUCTION II

As above, but the mistakes are simply underlined or circled, not coded or corrected.

H OTHER (If you have your own idea, write it here.)

Comments and grades

Think about the comments and the grading you would like to have. Again, be realistic. You might like to have three pages of comments, but your tutor or teacher doesn't have the time.

Some students don't like getting grades. If you do want a grade, you probably want a fairly simple system which tells you whether you are getting better. If you are a competitive person you may want a grade which tells you where you stand in relation to your group. For these a grade out of ten is probably best. This is a normal grading system:

9–10	Outstanding	A	5	Borderline	B–
8	Very good	A–	4	Poor	C
7	Good	B+	3	Weak	C–
6	OK	B	1–2	Very weak	D

If you want to know how you stand in relation to an examination you are aiming for, a Pass/Fail grade may be all you want.

Form

TASK 2

Now complete the form below, giving a brief indication of how you would like your feedback. Consult your teacher to see if this is acceptable. Finally, make some photocopies of the form and attach them to your future assignments.

KIND OF FEEDBACK WANTED

Tick (✓) the correction style you want.

MARKING	Errors corrected	
	Errors marked, but not corrected	
	Errors marked and coded but not corrected	
COMMENTS	General comments	
	Specific comments on one criterion (please specify)	
GRADE	No grade	
	Grade Pass/Fail	
	Grade 1–10	

Reading

Virtues and vices

The subject of your assignment is *virtues and vices*, so we have chosen an extract from a play which has plenty of them. Tennessee Williams' *A streetcar named Desire* is about a tragic and claustrophobic conflict of personalities, attitudes, lifestyles, values and interests. From the moment Blanche arrives to visit her sister Stella and meets Stella's husband Stanley, there is tension. Stanley has suspicions about what Blanche has done with Stella's family home; Blanche is horrified by Stanley's character and background. The personalities emerge vividly from the script, almost as irritating to us as they are to each other.

Here Stanley and Blanche are talking alone together the day after Blanche's arrival. Read the script aloud and try to give the words all the dramatic value they should have.

What kind of people are Stanley and Blanche?

Do you feel more sympathetic to one or the other?

Can you give a name to any of the feelings or traits they display?

ASSIGNMENT 4

For this assignment we are giving you a subject which is interesting and also easy to organize. It falls naturally into two parts.

> **Which virtues do you most admire?**
>
> **Which vices do you most deplore?**
>
> **Say why and illustrate from your own experience.**

Planning: notes

● Try a different layout for your notes this time.

Vices and Virtues	People	Behaviour

1   Think of some vices and virtues you admire and deplore.
2   At the same time, think of some people you admire or disapprove of.
3   Then think of some specific behaviour that you admire or deplore.
Write each thing you think of on a separate line in the table. There need be no connection between the three columns.
N.B.   *This is not an essay plan – it is just a way of freeing up your thinking and generating some ideas.*

● Now make some connections between the three columns. For example, you may have thought of a person you admire. Why? What virtues does s/he have? What specific behaviour?
● From your notes, select what you are going to write about. You probably don't want everything.
● Choose something which will make a good ending.
● Before you hand in your composition, do two things:
   1   give it to your reader and discuss it with him/her,
   2   attach a Feedback Form to the composition so your tutor/teacher knows what kind of feedback you want.

FEEDBACK

To the reader

Please complete this questionnaire.

	YES/NO
1 Has the writer met all seven document presentation requirements?	
2 Is the composition divided into two or more parts in some way – for example, one for vices and one for virtues? (If you can't see the basic organization, discuss this with the writer.)	
3 Select one thing in the composition that deserves a compliment – a phrase, an illustration, a good ending or beginning, an interesting fact, a useful new word. Write your compliment below.	

DIARY PROMPT

A student in an English class wanted to keep in touch with his classmates after the course was over. He assumed they were all too lazy to write letters, so as a joke he created an Annual Report Form which they could fill in to show what had happened to them over the previous year.

Fill in the form for yourself: its purpose is to make you think about what has happened to you over the last twelve months and give you some ideas for your diary – if you haven't any better ones.

ANNUAL REPORT FORM

Career/study progress

Number of steps a) backwards _____ b) forwards _____

Present situation _____

Adventures

a) romantic _____ b) other _____

Attitude development

	Up	Down
Materialism		
Vicious opportunism		
Disillusion		
Joie de vivre		
Anxiety/neurosis		
Saintliness		

State of body (strike out what does not apply)

fatter/thinner   healthier/sicker   smarter/shabbier
better/worse habits   recognizable/unrecognizable

State of English

defunct ☐   in cold storage ☐   limping along ☐
healthy and active ☐   razor sharp ☐

A STREETCAR NAMED DESIRE

(*Stanley is looking at Blanche's clothes.*)

Stanley	What does it cost for a string of fur-pieces like that?
Blanche	Why, those were a tribute from an admirer of mine!
Stanley	He must have had a lot of – admiration!
Blanche	Oh, in my youth I excited some admiration. But look at me now! (*She smiles at him radiantly.*) Would you think it possible that I was once considered to be – attractive?
Stanley	Your looks are okay.
Blanche	I was fishing for a compliment, Stanley.
Stanley	I don't go in for that stuff.
Blanche	What – stuff?
Stanley	Compliments to women about their looks. I never met a woman that didn't know if she was good-looking or not without being told, and some of them give themselves credit for more than they've got. I once went out with a doll who said to me, 'I am the glamorous type, I am the glamorous type!' I said, 'So what?'
Blanche	And what did she say then?
Stanley	She didn't say nothing. That shut her up like a clam.
Blanche	Did it end the romance?
Stanley	It ended the conversation – that was all. Some men are took in by this Hollywood glamour and some men are not.
Blanche	I'm sure you belong in the second category.
Stanley	That's right.
Blanche	I cannot imagine any witch of a woman casting a spell over you.
Stanley	That's – right.
Blanche	You're simple, straightforward and honest, a little bit on the primitive side, I should think. To interest you a woman would have to – (*She pauses with an indefinite gesture.*)
Stanley	(*Slowly*) Lay . . . her cards on the table.
Blanche	(*Smiling*) Well, I never cared for wishy-washy people. That was why, when you walked in here last night, I said to myself – 'My sister has married a man!' – Of course that was all that I could tell about you.
Stanley	(*Booming*) Now let's cut the re-bop!
Blanche	(*Pressing hands to her ears*): Ouuuuu! . . . All right; now, Mr Kowalski, let us proceed without any more double-talk. I'm ready to answer all questions. I've nothing to hide. What is it?
Stanley	There is such a thing in this State of Louisiana as the Napoleonic code, according to which whatever belongs to my wife is also mine – and vice versa.
Blanche	My, but you have an impressive judicial air! (*She sprays herself with her atomizer; then playfully sprays him with it. He seizes the atomizer and slams it down on the dresser. She throws back her head and laughs.*)
Stanley	If I didn't know that you was my wife's sister I'd get ideas about you!
Blanche	Such as what!
Stanley	Don't play so dumb. You know what!
Blanche	(*She puts the atomizer on the table.*) All right. Cards on the table. That suits me. (*She turns to Stanley.*) I know I fib a good deal. After all, a woman's charm is fifty per cent illusion, but when a thing is important I tell the truth, and this is the truth: I haven't cheated my sister or you or anyone else as long as I have lived.

Stanley	Where's the papers? In the trunk?
Blanche	Everything that I own is in that trunk.
	(*Stanley crosses to the trunk, shoves it roughly open and begins to open compartments.*)
Blanche	What in the name of heaven are you thinking of! What's in the back of that little boy's mind of yours? That I am absconding with something, attempting some kind of treachery on my sister? – Let me do that! It will be faster and simpler ... (*She crosses to the trunk and takes out a box.*) I keep my papers mostly in this tin box. (*She opens it.*)
Stanley	What's them underneath? (*He indicates another sheaf of papers.*)
Blanche	These are love-letters, yellowing with antiquity, all from one boy. (*He snatches them up. She speaks fiercely.*) Give those back to me!
Stanley	I'll have a look at them first!
Blanche	The touch of your hands insults them!
Stanley	Don't pull that stuff! (*He rips off the ribbon and starts to examine them. Blanche snatches them from him, and they cascade to the floor.*)
Blanche	Now that you've touched them, I'll burn them.
Stanley	(*Staring, baffled*) What in hell are they?
Blanche	(*On the floor gathering them up*) Poems a dead boy wrote. I hurt him the way that you would like to hurt me, but you can't! I'm not young and vulnerable any more. But my young husband was and I – never mind about that! Just give them back to me!
Stanley	What do you mean by saying you'll have to burn them?
Blanche	I'm sorry, I must have lost my head for a moment. Everyone has something he won't let others touch because of their – intimate nature ...
Stanley	I don't want any ifs, ands or buts! What's all the rest of them papers? (*She hands him the entire box. He carries it to the table and starts to examine the papers.*)
Stanley	I have a lawyer acquaintance who will study these out.
Blanche	Present them to him with a box of aspirin tablets.
Stanley	(*Becoming somewhat sheepish*) You see, under the Napoleonic code – a man has to take an interest in his wife's affairs – especially now that she's going to have a baby.
Blanche	Stella? Stella going to have a baby? (*Dreamily*) I didn't know she was going to have a baby! (*She gets up and crosses to the outside door. Stella appears around the corner. Stanley goes into the bedroom with the box. Blanche meets Stella at the foot of the steps of the sidewalk.*)
Blanche	Stella, Stella for star! How lovely to have a baby! It's all right. Everything's all right.
Stella	I'm sorry he did that to you.
Blanche	Oh, I guess he's just not the type that goes for jasmine perfume, but maybe he's what we need to mix our blood with now. We thrashed it out. I feel a bit shaky, but I think I handled it nicely, I laughed and treated it all as a joke. I called him a little boy and laughed and flirted. Yes, I was flirting with your husband! – Which way do we go now, Stella – this way?
Stella	No, this way. (*She leads Blanche away.*)
Blanche	(*Laughing*) The blind are leading the blind!

5 Language Preparation

! Look at Tests A and B for Unit 5, page 150 and 153.

Future possibilities

We would like to introduce you to some alternative ways of talking about future possibilities. *May* and *might* and *may well* are extremely common in English, but are not so often used by learners of English.

- *May* has the idea of **possibility**.
     We may go to Greece for our holidays. (It is possible that we will go.)
- Normally, *may* and *might* have almost the same meaning. But if you want to give the idea that there is only a small chance, you use *might*.
     We might even go on to Istanbul. (There is just a small chance.)
- *May well* has the idea of **probable** and also implies that this is a personal judgement.
     What do you think he'll say?
     Oh, he may well say nothing.
     (In my opinion it is probable that he will say nothing.)

1 To get used to using *may/might/may well*, read the following dialogue aloud with a partner. Use phrases with *may/might/may well* instead of the phrases *in italics* and make any other necessary changes.

A   What are Peter's chances of getting the job, would you say?
B   Well, in fact, *it's quite possible that Peter won't* apply.
A   Really?
B   Yes. It seems he's been approached by another firm and *it's possible that he'll* take that job instead.
A   But *it's also possible that he won't*?
B   That's right.
A   And Jack? What are his chances? He's applied, hasn't he?
B   Oh, yes. Well, it depends on who else applies. If they find someone really excellent, *it's quite possible that Jack won't* even get an interview.
A   But *perhaps they won't* be able to find anyone that good.
B   Well, in that case the board *will possibly* appoint Jack. Or *it's just possible that they will* leave the vacancy open.
A   So *there's just a chance we will* not have anyone in the post?
B   *Quite probably we will* not.
A   Or *perhaps they'll* put Jack in as a temporary manager?
   B   *That's possible* too.

2 Think of some real possibilities to complete the sentences below, as in the example. Use *may* or *might* or *may well*.

Example   If you apply for the course too late <u>you may well miss out</u>.

a   I've got some spare boots you could use somewhere, but _____

b   Put them in a bag, otherwise _____

c   We'd love to come to your party, but _____

d   I really think you shouldn't try to swim across. _____

_____

e   We should go and consult Mrs Redmond. _____

_____

f   DON'T press that red button, Sally! _____

Check with an expert.

Now, soon and recently

General expressions for *recently*, *now* and *soon* are often difficult because they are similar to (but not exactly the same as) those in your own language. There is a temptation to translate. Use the exercise below to diagnose which expressions you do not get exactly right, or don't know. (The exercise is full of gloom and grumbles – don't get depressed!)

3 Other ways of saying *recently* (one word for each space):

a   In the _____ _____ days the weather has been awful.

b   I haven't seen him so often _____.

c   In _____ years everyone has got greedier.

d   Hospital conditions have deteriorated of _____.

e   We all had a nasty shock not _____ _____.

Other ways of saying *now*:

f   You can never get a seat on a bus _____ days.

g   _____ , children spend all their time watching TV.

h   At _____ unemployment is increasing even faster.

i   There are no funds available at the _____ _____.

Other ways of saying *soon*:

j   There are no prospects for improvement in _____ _____ future.

k   The weather will _____ turn very cold.

l   We will all feel the effects in the _____ _____ months.

4 After checking the Key, practise the expressions by making your own grumbles about the recent past, present or near future – one of each if possible.

Prepositions

Remember to revise previous errors.

5
a   There is a great need _____ better publicity on AIDS.

b   There's no point _____ trying to talk to an idiot like him.

c   I am interested _____ almost everything.

d   I must point _____ that the answer is not simple.

e   The increase _____ sea pollution has reduced tourism here.

f   I heard it _____ the radio.

g   We don't want to make any changes _____ present.

h   This machine is nothing _____ trouble.

i   What's _____ the other channels?

j   I can manage perfectly well _____ myself.

  Check in the Key and rub out your mistakes.

6
● Look through all the previous preposition exercises to find expressions of *time* (there were six). What can you conclude?

● What about all those cases where no preposition was needed? There were six. What groups do they divide into?

  Check in the Key if you are not sure.

Spelling

Here we are talking about words ending in *y*. The problem is whether to keep the *y* when you add a suffix to the word. For example the *y* in *baby* changes to *ie* if you add the plural *s*: baby + s = babies,
but the *y* in *day* does not: day + s = days.

You need to concentrate only on the areas where you yourself make mistakes. To find out what these are, do the 'word sums' below, then check the answers. In the Key you will also find a short explanation of the rules.

7 Do these word sums.

a   happy   + er   = _____   g   study   + ed   = _____

b   employ + ed   = _____   h   die   + ing   = _____

c   day   + ly   = _____   i   supply + ed   = _____

d   copy   + ing   = _____   j   supply + ing   = _____

e   enjoy   + able   = _____   k   lie   + ing   = _____

f   study   + ing   = _____   l   pay   + ed   = _____

5 PARAGRAPHING

Writing Tutorial

There are two important questions about paragraphing:

layout What is a paragraph?
sense What are paragraphs for?

Let's start with layout.

What is a paragraph?

Layout

A paragraph in English is not quite the same as a paragraph in some other languages. These are paragraphs.

Don't read it, just look at it.

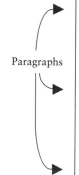

Paragraphs

'Imagine yourself alone and starving. You're on a cement street surrounded by cement buildings. The buildings have no doors and no windows. The street is endless. There's no hope. That's what a lost or abandoned pet, a dog or a cat, faces when it's turned loose in the city.'

Those words were spoken to me by a man from a charitable organization in Los Angeles called Delta. I got the message and couldn't wait to write him a cheque. I remembered some of the terrified animals I had seen in the streets and how my wife and I had tried to save them. He brought back those memories and moved me emotionally. He painted a picture I was unable to resist.

A truly effective 30-second message is more than a hook, a few words, and a close. Those words should paint a picture your listener will remember. They should be words your listener will understand. They should relate to your own and your listener's personal experiences. And they should reach your listener's heart.

There are three complete paragraphs in the text above.

A paragraph is something you can *see*. It starts away from the margin.

Starting away from the margin is called indentation. The paragraphs are indented. They start at a short distance from the margain set by the rest of the text.

Alternatively, the paragraph can start at the margin with the rest of the text, and be separated from the paragraph before by an empty line.

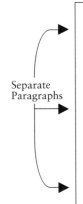

Paragraphs begin like this

```
    XXXXXXXXXXXXXXXXXXXXXXXXXXXXXXXXXXXXXXXXXXXXXXXXXXXXXXXX
    XXXXXXXXXXXXXXXXXXXXXXXXXXXXXXXXXXXXXXXXXXXXXXXXXXXXXXXX
    XXXXXXXXXXXXXXXXXXXX
       XXXXXXXXXXXXXXXXXXXXXXXXXXXXXXXXXXXXXXXXXXXXXXXXXXXXX
    XXXXXXXXXXXXXXXXXXXXXXXXXXXXXXXXXXXXXXXXXXXXXXXXXXXXXXXX
    XXXXXXXXXXXXXXXXXXXXXXXXXXXXXXXXXXXXXXXXXXXXXXXXXXXXXXXX
    XXXXXXXXXXXXXXXXXXXXXXXXXXXXXXXXXXXXXXXXXXXXXXXXXXXXXXXX
    XXXXXXXXXXXXXXXXXXXXXXXXXXXXXXXXXXXXXXXXXXXXXXXXXXXXXXXX
       XXXXXXXXXXXXXXXXXXXXXXXXXXXXXXXXXXXXXXXXXXXXXXXXXXXXX
    XXXXXXXXXXXXXXXXXXXXXXXXXXXXXXXXXXXXXXXXXXXXXXXXXXXXXXXX
    XXXXXXXXXXXXXXXXXXXXXXXXXXXXXXXXXXXXXXXXXXXXXXXXXXXXXXXX
    XXXXXXXXXXXXXXXXXXXXXXXXXXXXXXXXXXXXXXXXXXXXXXXXX
```

Separate Paragraphs

```
    XXXXXXXXXXXXXXXXXXXXXXXXXXXXXXXXXXXXXXXXXXXXXXXXXXXXXXXX
    XXXXXXXXXXXXXXXXXXXXXXXXXXXXXXXXXXXXXXXXXXXXXXXXXXXXXXXX
    XXXXXXXXXXXXXXXXXXXXXXXXXXXXXXXXXXXXXXXXXXXXX

    XXXXXXXXXXXXXXXXXXXXXXXXXXXXXXXXXXXXXXXXXXXXXXXXXXXXXXXX
    XXXXXXXXXXXXXXXXXXXXXXXXXXXXXXXXXXXXXXXXXXXXXXXXXXXXXXXX
    XXXXXXXXXXXXXXXXXXXXXXXXXXXXXXXXXXXXXXXXXXXXXXXXXXXXXXXX
    XXXXXXXXXXXXXXXXXXXXXXXXXXXXXXXXXXXXXXXXXXXXXXXXXXXXXXXX
    XXXXXXXXXXXXXXXXXXXXXXXXXXXXXXXXXXXXXXXXX

    XXXXXXXXXXXXXXXXXXXXXXXXXXXXXXXXXXXXXXXXXXXXXXXXXXXXXXXX
    XXXXXXXXXXXXXXXXXXXXXXXXXXXXXXXXXXXXXXXXXXXXXXXXXXXXXXXX
    XXXXXXXXXXXXXXXXXXXXXXXXXXXXXXXXXXXXXXXXXXXXXXXXXXXXXXXX
```

The paragraphs in the lower box are not indented.

ADVICE   *Since you are already writing your compositions double-spaced, we recommend that you indent your paragraphs.*

Paragraphs and sentences

A paragraph usually contains several sentences. It is possible to have a one-sentence paragraph, but these are quite rare.

Importance

Some languages are not very interested in paragraphs. By contrast, the world of normal written English is obsessed with paragraphs. (There is a reason, as we will see soon.)

As regards layout, the English therefore like all writing to be properly paragraphed according to the conventions we have described. They do not like:

– **no indentation,** where new paragraphs start at the margin so that you sometimes cannot be sure whether there is a new paragraph or not;

- **reverse indentation**, where the paragraph starts at the margin, but all the rest of the text is indented;
- **no paragraphing**, where the writing is not divided into paragraphs at all;
- **single-sentence paragraphs**, where there is one paragraph for every sentence.

TASK

1

Look back at the sample compositions in Unit 3, *Writing Tutorial* (pages 42–4). These are printed exactly as they were written, with their original paragraphing.
   Study the paragraphing layout in each case. Is it acceptable by the standards of normal written English? Apply the criteria above (*no indentation, reverse indentation* and so on). Write your comments below.

Composition

A _____

B _____

C _____

D _____

I think you will agree that none of them is completely acceptable.

Check in the Key if you are not sure what is wrong.

What are paragraphs for?

Sense

The philosophy is that each paragraph is about one main idea. This is the general idea – and *in general* it is true.
   Let's look at an example. On the next page is part of an article about asparagus. Read it quickly – don't bother *at all* about unknown words. As you come to each new paragraph, try to see what the new idea is.

ASPARAGUS is frequently mentioned in literature. Rabelais said it grew from seeds made of pulverised rams' horns. Proust was struck by the vegetable's heavenly flavour. And the noted 19th-century gourmet and writer Charles Monselet adored seeing the green tips mixed with 'the gold of scrambled egg'.

But asparagus also has beneficial diuretic properties. One quack of old claimed: 'Asparagus brings on women's periods, removes obstruction, and is very digestible. But it is not very nutritious.'

Now for the virtues of asparagus in the kitchen. It goes well with eggs, in an omelette, for example; scrambled eggs with asparagus tips are also good. You can even use an asparagus spear like a finger of toast and dip it into a boiled egg. Asparagus is also admirable in a soufflé or in a gratin, but I do wish chefs would refrain from adorning my plate with a few miserable asparagus tips (often straight out of a tin, believe it or not).

Asparagus really deserves to be eaten on its own. You peel the spears with a potato peeler, tie them up in a bundle and place them upright in boiling water in a narrow tall pan with their tips sticking two centimetres out of the water so they do not overcook.

The great question with boiled asparagus is: should it be eaten with a vinaigrette dressing or with melted butter? Thereby hangs a tale. The 18th-century writer, Bernard de Fontenelle, invited the Abbé Terrasson to lunch during the asparagus season. Fontenelle told his cook to prepare half the asparagus with butter, which is how the Abbé liked them, and half with an oil and vinegar dressing, his own preference.

While they were chatting away before the meal, the Abbé felt faint, then dropped dead. Fontenelle is alleged to have immediately shouted to the cook 'Oil with the lot! Oil with the lot!'

To finish, here is a recipe for asparagus which puts it in flattering company, that of the truffle. Sauté some thickly sliced truffles briskly in butter and mix with just-cooked asparagus tips. Deglaze the truffle pan with sherry and a little of the asparagus water, and pour over the mixture. Sprinkle with chopped chervil.

Guardian Weekly 10.6.90

TASK 2

The subjects of the paragraphs (not in the right order) are:

1 The medical value of asparagus
2 A recipe for asparagus
3 How to cook asparagus
4 Asparagus with other food
5 Asparagus in literature
6 What kind of dressing goes with asparagus
   (One other paragraph is used to make a narrative break in the anecdote.)

  Look through the article and write the appropriate number next to each paragraph.

TASK 3

On page 75 is a well-paragraphed composition. The structure is simple but very clear. Read it through and work out what is the idea of each paragraph. Try to see how each paragraph relates to the others. You should get some help from the title. Write the subjects of the paragraphs below.

Paragraph 1 _____

Paragraph 2 _____

Paragraph 3 _____

> ### A CAREER: IMAGE AND REALITY
>
> *People imagine strange things about a 'glamour career'. For example, of a business tycoon they think he is a lucky man: he can travel, he has a lot of money, a beautiful car, he lives in a villa with a swimming-pool. His life is busy with parties, galas, important anniversaries. Beautiful women fall at his feet, his friends are important people like movie and TV stars, politicians and men of the financial world. All he dreams can become reality.*
>
> *This is very silly. In reality, a top business man has no private life. Reporters, journalists are always intruding on his life, the lights are always on his face. He has to work hard to maintain his power; he probably risks his wealth every day as he does business. Life is demanding: he has to be very intelligent to understand where the wind of affairs is blowing. Quite probably the beautiful women he meets only want his money, jewels, furs, expensive holidays; he must have difficulties having normal relationships with people.*
>
> *However, what constitutes the glamour of such a man is not only the reality but the dream as well. Martinelli, in his book 'Portraits', says that the first money which Rizzoli managed to get for his firm was from a bank manager who believed more in the 'glamour' of Rizzoli's ideas than in the reality – for Rizzoli had no money. So is a tycoon always tired of his glamour? I think not. I think the image of any powerful man is not simply false: it is also a part of his work and life.*

You will see how each paragraph in the composition deals with a separate point, and how all the points are related to each other.

Clearly, it is difficult to paragraph well unless your writing is well organized, with each idea treated separately. (We'll come back to this later in the course.) Most students' writing is not very badly organized. It simply needs paragraphing to make the organization clear to the reader – and sometimes also to the writer.

> *THE MESSAGE for you as a writer is: when you feel you are moving on to a new point, start a new paragraph.*

On the next page are two compositions which are essentially well-organized but need improved paragraphing.

TASK 4   The first already has some paragraphing. It needs a little more. If you were revising it, where would you make the breaks? Mark the text with NP (new paragraph).

TASK 5   The second has too many paragraphs – one for each sentence. Show how you would group the sentences into paragraphs.

BEING A FIRST LADY: IMAGE AND REALITY

Generally, most people – above all, girls – dream of a fabulous future. They would like to meet a beautiful boy, a prince, a king, and they therefore identify themselves with Lady Diana, or Princess Grace of Monaco, Prince Rainier's wife.

Girls, when they read magazines about these people, think that a first lady is lucky. She is always surrounded by people who help her in her daily life. They are the cook, the domestic servant, the butler and the nanny who looks after the children. In fact, when she goes out she can leave her house and her children without any problem. A first lady is always busy. She has appointments she must keep. She has to go to parties and to the theatre. She passes her weekends in wonderful places and in the summer she goes to Greece, Sardinia, the Seychelles with her family. Another reason girls dream of being a first lady is because she always wears beautiful clothes and jewels.

The reality is different. Certainly, a first lady is rich and successful but she has no private life. Magazines look for news and pictures about her and show her in moments of her private life. People are always watching her and she must always be perfect, smiling and elegant. Then, she must always follow her husband, and if she is a career woman she must give it up and help her husband. Grace Kelly was an example: in fact she left her movie career to marry Prince Rainier.

In short, it is important to remember that there is no rose without a thorn!

YES, I DO WANT TO LOCK UP THE TERRORISTS

Some terrorists in prison today have a lot of privileges.

For example, they can leave jail and go to work and then go back to the cell to spend the night.

Many people think that it is right for prisoners to leave the jail in this way, so they have the chance to reinstate themselves in the society that they rejected before.

I do not agree with this opinion.

I may seem a bit categorical about this topic but I think that if a person commits any kind of crime in his life he has to pay his debt to society.

If he is allowed to live like a free person, he will never understand what he has done wrong.

In this case, his repentance cannot be considered to be real.

I think that if life in jail was not so comfortable everybody would think twice before committing a crime.

Reading

Beware the Eurogook

The article at the end of this unit shows a fine example of active feedback at work. Chrissie Maher suffered personally from the elaborate and obscure language in official forms and documents. She reacted to it by starting the Plain English Campaign, and she made the official world listen to her and change their ways. The campaign made such an impact that thousands of forms were abolished and thousands more were improved.

Before writing your assignment, you may want to take a look at Chrissie Maher's tactics and strategies and discuss why they worked.

ASSIGNMENT 5

CAMPAIGN

Is there something you would like to see reformed or changed in your town or country?
  What ?
  Why ?
  What is your personal interest?

● **Give details.**

  How would you start - and maintain - a campaign for the kind of change you want to see? What would you hope to achieve?

● **Describe your strategy, step by step.**

Planning: getting ideas

This is a composition where you need a *practical* imagination.

● Think of two or three subjects for your campaign, things that you personally want to change, then select the best. Choose something small and realistic: it would be nice to abolish war, for example, but you would have more chance with reducing the waiting-list for telephones or planting more trees in the suburbs.

● Spend time thinking how you would do it. The initiative is all yours – it is no good saying that someone else should act. Where will you try to apply pressure? You will need money: how will you raise it? You will not be able to do much alone: what organizations can you use – or create?

● Pay attention to paragraphing. This composition is easy to divide into two parts:
  a   the description of the *problem*, and
  b   the steps towards a *solution*.

● Attach a feedback form to your finished composition.

FEEDBACK

To the reader

Please complete this questionnaire.

		YES/NO
1	Are all the document presentation requirements met?	
2	Is the composition physically paragraphed?	
3	Are the paragraphs correctly laid out?	
4	Can the composition be divided clearly into two or more parts?	
5	Do the paragraphs reflect the parts?	
6	Is the reform really needed?	
7	Is the campaign described feasible? Will it work?	
8	Describe one thing you liked in the composition.	

DIARY PROMPT

What are the three best films/TV programmes you have seen in your whole life – the ones you remember vividly? Why did they impress you so much?

Beware the eurogook...

Chrissie Maher could not read and write properly until she was sixteen. Today, this 'fast-talking Scouse grandmother' and her business partner Martin Cutts are consulted on matters of good English by government departments, local councils, banks, insurance companies and businesses large and small who support the Plain English Campaign. **SYLVIA CHALKER reports.**

The Campaign grew directly from Chrissie Maher's own personal experience. When she finally became literate she found that many forms, agreements and official letters were in fact unreadable – with the result that many people were seriously losing out. People entitled to welfare benefits were not applying because they did not understand the forms; people were having accidents with medicines because of bad labelling; there was even a couple who lost their home because they had not understood the rental purchase agreement they had signed.

After several years of confronting such problems while running a community newspaper and working for the National Consumer Council, Chrissie decided with Martin Cutts to launch an all-out attack on "jargon, legal language and small print". The attack began in 1979.

One July day that year a strange scene met the eyes of people passing through Parliament Square, London – just around the corner from many government offices in Whitehall. Chrissie Maher and Martin Cutts were ritually shredding piles of official government forms.

The story goes that the pair only narrowly escaped arrest on this occasion for their lèse-majesté. But the media loved it and it struck a chord not only with the form-filling public, but also with the Thatcher government, who were keen to modernise the Civil Service. In 1982 a government White Paper told departments to abolish all unnecessary forms and improve the rest.

Two early triumphs were a much simplified tax form for basic-rate taxpayers, and a television licence form which no longer burbled about "hereinafter called the licensee" or "apparatus for wireless telegraphy". Further notable success came in 1984 when the Campaign was called in as a consultant to the Cabinet Office to help produce *The Word is Plain English*, an advisory booklet for over 20,000 civil servants.

By 1985 more than 15,000 official forms had disappeared, a further 21,300 had been drastically revised and government ministers were attending a Plain English exhibition in Whitehall. The following year there was an exhibition at the House of Commons, and in 1989, when the Campaign celebrated its tenth anniversary, there was a pledge from the Prime Minister to continue to "banish jargon and officialese from government documents".

In the past decade, the Plain English Campaign has established itself as something of a power in the land. But though it is delighted to have government approval, it is an entirely independent organization. It finances its campaigning through training courses, a consultancy service and a range of publications that includes an anthology of awful officialese, called simply *Gobbledygook*.

As PEC enters the 1990s, the war on verbiage continues, on an extended battleground. Chrissie Maher recently discovered a European Community document with an opening sentence of 1,842 words. If Eurospeak is to shed its Gookspeak image, PEC is in for another busy ten years.

6 Language Preparation

! Look at Tests A and B for Unit 6, pages 150 and 153.

Most, all, some

Check that you know all these points about *most*, *all* and *some* – in practice, not just in theory. If you are sure you do, perhaps you don't need the exercises.

		Do you know it?

1 All	● The general sense has no *the*, e.g.
	    all black cats are lucky
	    all sport is competitive
	    NOT 'All the black cats . . .'
	
	● You don't usually say *all people* or *all things* or *all*. In modern English you say *everyone/everybody* and *everything*.	

2 Most	● The general sense has no *the*, e.g.
	    most people like good food
	    most paper is made from wood
	    NOT 'Most of the people . . .'
	
	● An alternative for *most* is *the majority of*, but this is only for plurals, e.g.
	    the majority *of* voters,
	    the majority *of* votes.
	    Most is much more common.	

3 Some	● The general sense has no *the*, e.g.
	    some spiders are poisonous
	    we need **some boiling water**
	    NOT 'Some of the spiders . . .'
	
	● If you are talking about people's opinions or behaviour in general, you do not use *someone*.
	
	Instead you can say *some people*, e.g.
	    some people hate spiders
	
	Or, in a semi-formal style, you can write just *some*, e.g.
	    some think this is a mistake;
	    others disagree	

There is a communication problem in this conversation. Can you explain it?

Carlo   All the old people love Bogart movies.
Neil   Oh, yeah . . . which old people are you thinking of?
Carlo   *All* the old people.
Neil   You know a lot of old people, do you?
Carlo   No, no, *all* the old people. Everywhere.
Neil   Oh, I see. You mean *all* of them.

Carlo   That's what I said!!

In the passage below the uses of *all* have an old-fashioned sound. Can you replace them with something more modern?

All people avoided the old factory. Some said that it was haunted: that the night watchman who had been killed there still walked around it at night when *all* was dark. Not *all people* agreed with this story. In particular, Joe thought it was rubbish, and said so. But in spite of *all that* he said, he was just like *all other people* – he too never went near the factory.

Finally, make six general statements (which you think are true) from the table below. Try to make them controversial. Then find someone who disagrees with you and try to reach a compromise position.

Gender stereotypes

All Most Some The majority of	people men/ boys women/ girls	hate(s) going to the dentist like(s) sports want(s) to have children is/are vain is/are aggressive hate(s) washing and ironing think(s) their work is important want(s) to be looked after
Everyone		like(s) chocolate is/are sentimental want(s) love and affection is/are very competitive

People and their kids

The words for people often need sorting out. As you read the points below, check whether you know them.

	Yes (known)
1 *People* is the general word – and it is plural. People *are, do, have* (**not** *is, does, has*).	
2 *Kids* is the colloquial word for young children.	
3 *Children* is the general word for young people under the age of about 12, i.e. anyone who is not yet a teenager.	
4 *Children* is also used for people of any age in relation to their parents. You are your parents' child, even when you are 80.	
5 *Sons* and *boys* are only male. Their female equivalents are *daughters* and *girls*. So if someone has three children, one female and two male, you would say 'She has two sons and a daughter', **not** 'She has three sons'.	
6 A mixed group of young people cannot be called 'boys' if they are boys *and* girls. Nor can you call them 'youngs', because *young* is not a noun. You can only call them *young people*, (or *boys and girls* if they are young enough).	
7 *Nephews* and *nieces* are only the sons and daughters of your brothers and sisters, **not** your children's children.	
8 Your children's children are your *grandchildren*, **not** your nephews and nieces. The boys are *grandsons* and the girls are *granddaughters*.	
9 Many women object to women being called *girls* (which happens much more often than men being called *boys*).	

Study the family tree below and refer back to the table. Then fill in the spaces.

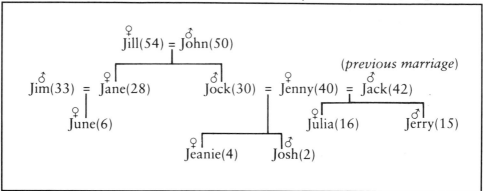

a   There are twelve _____ in this chart.

b   Jane and Jock are Jill's _____ , but they are not _____ now.

c   Julia and Jerry had a party for their friends. There were thirteen _____ there.

d   Jenny has two _____ and two _____ .

e   She has four _____ .

f   Jeanie and Josh are much younger than Julia and Jerry. Jeanie and Josh are still _____ , while Julia and Jerry are _____ .

g   Jim thinks one _____ is quite enough, but Jane would like to have a _____ to balance the family.

h   Jock and Jenny don't want to have any more _____ .

i   Jill and John send presents to their five young _____ .

j   In the third generation there are three _____ and two _____ .

k   Jock has a six-year-old _____ .

 l   Josh is John's youngest _____ and also Jane's _____ .

Prepositions

Revise your previous mistakes, and go on working in pencil. Remember that sometimes no preposition is needed.

a   I have never been able to find _____ where they live.

b   Workers of the world! You have nothing to lose _____ your chains.

c   We took all the boxes _____ the shelf and then cleaned it.

d   It's no use _____ drinking decaffeinated coffee: it doesn't wake you up.

e   Some political groups want to go back _____ the past.

f   Can you do it _____ your own? Do you need some help?

g   I have often wished _____ a more beautiful nose.

h   I am extremely good _____ learning languages.

i   There has been no change _____ her condition since she went to hospital.

j   Some faces look completely different when you see them _____ the screen.

Check in the Key and rub out your errors.

6   Look back at previous preposition exercises and find all the prepositions associated with the *mass media* (there are seven). Can you work out any rules?

Punctuation

It is possible that you are not using the full range of punctuation available to you in English (. , ; – :).

7   Consider what punctuation to use at the points marked □ in the passage below.

When I got home there was a message on the telephone answering machine [1]□ Cleo wanted me to go to the cinema. I felt annoyed [2]□ I didn't want to go out. It wasn't that I didn't like Cleo [3]□ she was my best friend [4]□ but I was tired [5]□ I had done too much already that day.

Check in the Key to see what punctuation is possible.

8   If you have found that there is some punctuation you do not normally use, experiment with it in the rest of the passage below.

But there was a problem. I couldn't just ring Cleo and say that I was tired. The reason was simple [1]□ I had said no to Cleo's last three invitations. She would certainly be hurt if I did it again [2]□ she was a sensitive person. Eventually I decided to ignore the message [3]□ just pretend I hadn't received it. That's the beauty of an answering machine [4]□ it tells your lies for you.

6 WHAT TO SAY

Writing Tutorial

Suppose this is an examination and you have to write a composition. There you are, sitting at your desk, staring at the subject. It does not inspire one single thought. You have nothing to say. You have to write 250 words about it. What do you do?

First, *don't* start writing. You will probably stop after a few lines and feel even more desperate. This is what you can do.

1 Get some ideas.
2 Select the ones which go together and throw away the rest.
3 Decide how you are going to end.
4 Start writing.

Getting ideas

The ideas are there, in your head. It is just that they are not always accessible; you cannot get at them. To do this you have to shake up your brain. We will call this *brainracking*. (Doing this in groups is called *brainstorming*. We have invented the term *brainracking*. It comes from 'racking one's brains'.)

Brainracking is like dropping stones into a pond to stir it up. You throw questions and associations into your head until something comes out. The idea is simply to make links between the subject and your knowledge and experience. All sorts of questions and associations can help.

When you need to get ideas, go through a routine like the following.

1 **Me and the subject** What experience do you personally have? Where does this subject touch *you*? What is your attitude to it? Does everyone think/ feel as you do? It is easier to write about things that interest you. Make (and remember) a list of some things that really interest you (e.g. *football, flamenco guitar, the mafia*) and make links between them and the subject. By making links you control what you write about.

2 **Take a position** Is the composition about a question of opinion? If so, decide immediately what your opinion is ('I think ...'). Then imagine someone you know disagreeing with you.

3 **Find examples and illustrations** Think of *real* examples, things which you know about, things which have happened to you or to people you know, things you have seen.

4 **Ask questions** Try inventing questions about the subject. Not all questions will work (it depends on the subject) but that doesn't matter. Ask *why, what, who, where, how,* and answer those questions.

5   **Compare** Whatever the subject is, think about:
  –   how it is different from others
  –   how it was different in the past
  –   how it will be different in the future
  –   how it is different in other places or other countries.

6   **Culture** Think of the subject in literature, art, films, TV, and the news.

Examples

Below and on the next page of this unit there are two examples (A and B) of people thinking onto paper in this way. The subject was *trees*.

These two people think quite differently. One is more *divergent*: unconnected ideas all over the page. The other is more *convergent*: ideas coming together in a list, concentrated on one aspect at a time. Take a look at them.

TASK

1   First of all, which is which?
2   Which one is already half planned?
3   In Example A, the order in which the writer thought of the ideas is shown by numbers. What was the first idea to come? And the second? And the third? And the fourth?

EXAMPLE A

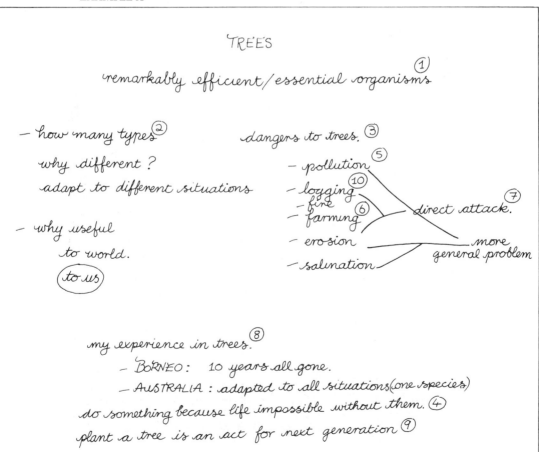

EXAMPLE B

The answers to this exercise do not matter very much. The idea of doing it is to help you to notice two important facts:
● there are many different ways of putting ideas onto paper and none of them is right or wrong;
● *nobody* plans a composition in a straight line, from beginning to end – even if the result is a list.

TASK 2

Below is a checklist for brainracking. This is how you use it.
1   Take a separate piece of paper – large, empty, unlined.
2   Take the subject of the composition and go through all the points on the checklist. (Some of them will not produce any ideas – that doesn't matter.)
3   Write down *all* the ideas that come to you. Write them anywhere on the paper. Spread yourself. Use the paper as a big field to lay out your ideas. Draw pictures, write sideways, write big or small. Feel free.

For this exercise, you have a choice of two subjects: **a Mice** or   **b Mountains**.

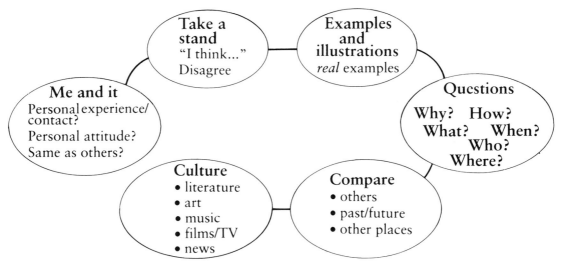

ADVICE   *Work in a small group if possible. It is more interesting and productive.*

Selecting

Getting a lot of ideas is just the beginning. The purpose of racking your brain is to get one good idea. The others you throw away.

TASK 3

Look at Example B again. This writer has plenty of ideas, but there are too many and they are very unconnected. She needs to find a few which go together and forget about the rest. Which ideas in Example B go together and could become the *main idea* of a composition?
    One is the ideas of *trees in the background* (in life, literature and art). This includes the points about Renaissance art, Shakespeare, Dutch Elm Disease and writing about trees.
Find two more.

1   _____

2   _____

TASK 4

Do the same with your own ideas. Choose *one* main idea from the ones you had about mice or mountains, and say goodbye to all the others.

Obviously, your main idea must be big enough to include several of your other points. It should be the centre of a group of ideas.

Which idea would you select?

_____

_____

Decide on the ending

Finally, *before* you start writing, decide on your ending. Ending is the difficult bit, so it is a good idea to have an ending to work towards, even if you change your mind later.

Choose something good. Often writers start with their best ideas – but they should think of the ending too. The ending is the climax; it is what your readers remember. Your ending should be *closely connected with your main idea*.

TASK 5

How would you end your composition on mice or mountains?

_____

_____

Reading

The Green Hat

A student once asked me 'How can I have ideas if I don't have any imagination?' I thought it was a very good question.

Edward de Bono, who wrote the text at the end of this unit, would say that people can *learn* to be imaginative, that it is a question of practice, like all other kinds of thinking. De Bono is probably the world's best-known writer on the teaching of thinking. He invented the idea of 'lateral thinking' – that is, generating ideas by going *sideways and around* a subject. Brainracking is a version of lateral thinking.

De Bono's recent book *Six Thinking Hats* describes six different kinds of thinking, each represented by a different coloured hat. White hat thinking is about objective facts, black hat thinking is critical, often negative, yellow hat thinking makes positive comments, red hat thinking is about feelings and emotional responses, and blue hat thinking co-ordinates all the other kinds of thinking. Your text is about the green hat – lateral and creative thinking.

All De Bono's writing is intended to change people's behaviour and ideas. So, as you read, think what it means for *you*. What does he advise you to do? What does he tell you that is different from the way you thought before?

When you have finished, write down in one or two sentences what message it has for your behaviour. Then discuss it with others if possible.

ASSIGNMENT 6

We are giving you five wide-open subjects to write about, including the two you have already thought about.

*Your purpose is to find something you really want to say about **one** of them, and write a composition in which we can hear your voice speaking.*

*Choose **one** of these:*

- **Mice**
- **Mountains**
- **Men**
- **Military service**
- **Mushrooms**

Feedback work

Before you start the composition, do some feedback work on your previous assignment.

Planning: selection

- Even if you already have some ideas, go through the brainracking process anyway. Remember: the aim is to find something you want to say – not to release more hot air into the atmosphere.
- From the ideas you generate, select one good one which includes several other points. *Forget all the others* – they may be rich but they are not relevant.
- Decide on the ending.
- Start writing. Stick to your main idea.

FEEDBACK

To the reader

Please complete this checklist.

Does the composition follow the document presentation requirements? (Yes/No)	
Is it laid out in paragraphs? (Yes/No)	
How many ideas are there? (Count them.)	
Is the writing stronger on range or on accuracy?	
What aspect of the composition do you like best?	
Please make one suggestion for improvement.	

DIARY PROMPT

This photograph belonged to a Puerto Rican boy living in New York's Lower East Side. His words are below.

I was about sixteen years old, I figured I was bad in the street, so I guess that's why I wanted to buy a gun for my son, so he could protect himself when he grows up, so nobody messed with him.

Then I started thinking that's wrong, you have to be a maniac to buy a gun for a kid like that. I talked to a couple of people and they made me sell it. They taught me something, you know?

Find a photograph that means a lot to you personally, or one that has a story attached, and write about it. If you are going to show your diary to someone, photocopy your photograph.

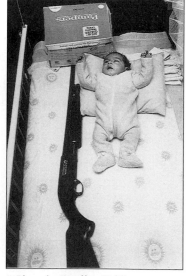

© Photo by Geoffrey Biddle.

THE GREEN HAT

Creative and lateral thinking

New ideas, new concepts and new perceptions
The deliberate creation of new ideas
Alternatives and more alternatives
Change
New approaches to problems

Green is the colour of fertility and growth and plants that grow from tiny seeds. That is why I chose green as the symbolic color for the thinking hat that is specifically concerned with creativity. The abundant creativity of nature is a useful background image.

The green thinking hat is specifically concerned with new ideas and new ways of looking at things. Green hat thinking is concerned with escaping from the old ideas in order to find better ones. Green hat thinking is concerned with change. Green hat thinking is a deliberate and focused effort in this direction.

'*... Let's have some new ideas on this. Put on your green thinking hats.*'

'*... We are bogged down. We keep going over the same old ideas. We desperately need a new approach. The time has come for some deliberate green thinking. Let's go.*'

'*... You have laid out the traditional approaches to this problem. We shall come back to them. But first let us have ten minutes of green hat thinking to see if we can come up with a fresh approach.*'

'*... This demands a green hat solution.*'

We need creativity because nothing else has worked.

There are times when we need to use creativity in a deliberate and focused manner. The green hat allows us to switch into the creative role, just as the red hat allows us to switch into the 'feeling' role and the black hat into the negative role.

In fact, there may be more need for the green hat than for any other of the thinking hats. It is particularly important to use the green hat as a *signal to yourself*. You deliberately put on the green hat, and this means that you are setting aside time for deliberate creative thinking. This is quite different from simply waiting for ideas to come to you. You may have no new ideas at all while wearing the green hat, but the effort has been made. As you get better at deliberate creative thinking, you will find that the yield of ideas increases. In this way the green hat makes creative thinking a formal part of the thinking process instead of just a luxury.

For most people the idiom of creative thinking is difficult because it is contrary to the natural habits of recognition, judgement and criticism. The brain is designed as a 'recognition machine'. It is designed to set up patterns, to use them and to condemn anything that does not 'fit' these patterns. Most thinkers like to be secure. They like to be right. Creativity involves provocation, exploration and risk taking. Creativity involves 'thought experiments'. You cannot tell in advance how the experiment is going to turn out. But you want to be able to carry out the experiment.

> '... *My green hat contribution is to suggest that we pay long-stay prisoners a decent pension on their discharge. That could help them get back into society, give them something to lose and prevent them from having to go back to crime.*'

> '... *Under the protection of the green hat, I want to suggest that we fire the sales force.*'

The green hat by itself cannot make people more creative. The green hat can, however, give thinkers the time and focus to be more creative. If you spend more time searching for alternatives, you are likely to find more. The green hat device allows a sort of artificial motivation.

Creativity is more than just being positive and optimistic. Positive and optimistic feelings fit under the red hat. Positive assessment fits under the yellow hat. Green hat thinking demands actual new ideas, new approaches and further alternatives.

With white hat thinking we do expect a definite input of neutral and objective information. With black hat thinking we do expect some specific criticisms. With yellow hat thinking we would like to get positive comments, but this may not always be possible. With red hat thinking we do expect to get a report on the feelings involved even if these are neutral. With green hat thinking, however, we cannot *demand* an input. We can only demand an effort. We can demand that time be set aside for generating new ideas.

You cannot order yourself (or others) to have a new idea, but you can order yourself (or others) to spend time trying to have a new idea. The green hat provides a formal way of doing this.

7 Language Preparation

!   Look at Tests A and B for Unit 7, pages 151 and 153.

Speech to writing

When you move from speech to writing, and from a colloquial to a semi-formal style, there are a few small changes you regularly have to make.

- *Have got* belongs mainly to *informal* spoken English. In semi-formal written English, you should in general use *have*, *does not have*, *did not have*, etc.
- **Contractions**, for example *can't, don't, it's, I'm*, in general are **not** used in the semi-formal style, and you should start to use them less in compositions.
- *Not/No* When you abandon contractions, other problems arise. For example, take the sentence: *There aren't any real solutions to this problem.* Without the contraction, you have to write: *There are not any real solutions to this problem.* But this doesn't sound English. So you must say: *There are no real solutions to this problem.* This happens with several verbs.

Informal	Semi-formal
There hasn't been any change. →	*There has been **no** change.*
I haven't got any money. →	*I have **no** money.*
I don't see any reason … →	*I see **no** reason …*

But it is only really essential with the verb *to be*.

Below is a composition. Edit it so that it sounds like semi-formal written English.

> A long time ago there weren't any cars. We can't say that there weren't any accidents in those days, as it was always possible for a cart or a chariot to hit something or somebody, but at least there wasn't any pollution.
>
> Nowadays, by contrast, everyone's got a car and as a result it isn't any longer possible to walk in the streets or to breathe clean air. Moreover, air pollution doesn't only affect people: it's also damaging the stone and metal of buildings and statues. For example, our cathedral's walls are black and dirty, but the cost of cleaning them is enormous. There was a magnificent bronze equestrian statue in the main square of our town but now it's been removed for restoration. Possibly we'll never see it again. But the statue is lucky. For the little stone faces on the cathedral walls there isn't any remedy: they've already lost their noses, and this has happened in just the last twenty years.
>
> I haven't got a car myself, and I feel that I'm being sacrificed for the people who have. Before my nose disappears as well, I want to say 'NO MORE CARS! NO MORE POLLUTION! LET ME BREATHE!'

Emphasis

What are the words you use to make a point stronger?
Suppose this is your plain simple idea:

Good short compositions
are not easy to write.

There are two things you can do:

1   You can make the idea more **emphatic**.
    For example:
    Good short compositions are
    not at all easy to write.
    Good short compositions are
    certainly not easy to write.
    Good short compositions are
    undoubtedly not easy to write.

Good short compositions
are not easy to write.

! Find out the pronunciation of *undoubtedly*.

2   You can point to the **idea**.

Good short compositions
are not easy to write.

I would like to	**emphasize**	that good short compositions
I want to	**point out**	are not easy to write.
It is important to	**stress**	

Normal emphasis is conveyed by words like *very*, *big* and *a lot*. More
formal alternatives are:

very	=	extremely, remarkably, unusually
		(*an extremely/remarkably/unusually hot summer*)
big	=	considerable, great
		(*a considerable/great increase*)
a lot of	=	a large number of, a great deal of
		(*a large number of songs, a great deal of luck*)

2   Rewrite the paragraph below to make it more emphatic and enthusiastic, and
also more formal. Use the suggestions above and anything else that you think is
appropriate. It is not easy to get this right, so check it with an expert when you
have finished.

*Mr Longbotham has always been very friendly, and has helped us to settle into
our new home. When we arrived in the street, we did not have any furniture and Mr
Longbotham went to a lot of trouble to find some for us. If it was not for him, we
would still be sitting on the floor. He has done us a lot of favours and we will
always be grateful to him. So I find it very difficult to believe that he is a mass
murderer.*

Prepositions

Revise as usual, and continue in pencil.

▼ 3

a   They have turned down our request _____ financial help.

b   Why are some children bad _____ mathematics at school?

c   She's wonderful – she can cope _____ anything.

d   These plants are greatly affected by a drop _____ temperature.

e   He wanted to stress _____ the fact that it wasn't his fault.

f   It's no good _____ trying to convince him: he won't listen.

g   We succeeded _____ rescuing three of the puppies.

h   _____ general, people like eating – but my brother doesn't.

i   They have a deep belief _____ democracy.

O—ᴛᴛ j   Take me _____ home at once.

▼ 4

Go through previous preposition exercises and find:
  – nouns for *needs* and *desires* (there are four). What is the preposition that goes with the nouns?
  – expressions of *futility* (there are three). What can you conclude about the prepositions in them?

O—ᴛᴛ

Spelling

Three words which are easily confused are **choose**, **chose** and **choice**.
First get the pronunciation right. Look in the dictionary or ask an expert.
Then establish which word is which.
The past tense _____
The noun _____
The present tense/infinitive _____

▼ 5

Put the right *form* of the right word in the spaces.

The fact was that I had too many [1]_____ . I could [2]_____ Fanny, the domesticated one, or Becky, the career woman, or Mary the model. If I [3]_____ Fanny, I would eat well for life. If my [4]_____ was Becky, I could probably stop work since she would always earn enough money for both of us. [5]_____ Mary would mean always having something decorative to look at. Put that way, it was a [6]_____ between comfort, idleness and aesthetics. In the end I [7]_____ idleness.

O—ᴛᴛ

7 STYLE

Writing Tutorial

The semi-formal style

You are aiming for a semi-formal style, not too colloquial and not too elaborate. This is really not much of a problem. We have only a few guidelines for you.

What to avoid (1)

Some languages have a *high style*, a rather elaborate poetic language usually associated with the arts, or learning, or the cultural heritage. Here is a sample.

> *Dark and tempestuous was the night. Around the throne on high not a single star quivered, but the deep intonations of the heavy thunder constantly vibrated upon the ear, whilst the terrific lightning revelled in angry mood through the cloudy chambers of the heaven. Even the boisterous winds unanimously came forth from the mystic homes, and blustered about as if to enhance by their aid the wildness of the scene ...*
>
> From *Tom Sawyer* by Mark Twain

If your language has a high style, then beware of trying to translate it into modern English – because English no longer has a style of this kind. It has faded away.

Equally, if you are able to write the high style in your own language, don't try to do it in English: it doesn't work. You will have to learn other ways of being impressive – more English ways.

At the same time, you must also avoid *over-colloquial language*. Here is an over-colloquial opening.

> 'My brother-in-law Joe is a <u>really</u> nice guy, no kidding!'

This style is fine for a letter to a friend, but it is a bit too informal for a composition. In a semi-formal style you would need to change the vocabulary and take out the underlining and the exclamation mark.

> 'My brother-in-law Joe is really an amazingly nice person.'

Or, you could be even more formal.

> 'My brother-in-law Joe has an extraordinarily attractive personality.'

Over-colloquial language will not be a problem for you if you don't yet know much colloquial language. But it is sometimes a danger for those who have been abroad and learnt to speak colloquial English, but have not had much practice writing semi-formal English.

Speech to writing

At this point in your writing career you need to start moving away from writing spoken English. Let's look at an example. Here is a piece of writing about abortion.

Version A

> *No, I think abortion is wrong. I really hate the idea. It's killing a person. It horrifies me. Anyway, it shouldn't be necessary. These days you don't have to get pregnant. Why don't people take precautions so they don't have to take away a life? We don't have the right to take away a human life. Some people say it's not a human life but I think it is.*

Don't be distracted by the content. Whether or not we agree with the opinion, we must say that the English is good. However, it is almost exactly like spoken English. Now look at the same content, re-written in a slightly more formal style.

Version B

> *Abortion to me means killing a person, taking away a human life. I find this horrifying and I feel we have no right to do it. I think people should take precautions so that they are not faced with this choice.*

TASK 1   How does **Version B** differ from **Version A**? Make a few notes on the differences.

The words   _____

_____

The sentences _____

_____

The organization _____

_____

Check in the Key if you are not certain about all the differences.

You can see that semi-formal style is still close to the spoken language, but it
- – is more thoughtful
- – is more precise
- – is more complex
- – is more synthetic
- – is better organized
- – has more authority
- – uses a wider range of language.

TASK 2

Here are two more pairs of texts – the same ideas written in both the semi-formal style and in *spoken English style*. Read them and decide which is which.

A1   *I like travelling but I've never gone far. I like travel because it is exciting but I also like it because it relaxes you. I suppose I want both. I want to relax and I want to learn something.*

A2   *I've always enjoyed travelling, though I've never gone far. However, my ideal journey would be to a place which would be relaxing and stimulating at the same time, so that I could have a rest and learn something interesting as well.*

B1   *I feel it is fundamentally wrong for a person to spend his whole life in prison. I agree that a criminal who has been found guilty should pay for his crime, but I think this should be only for a year or two, and after this he should be released.*

B2   *I don't think it's right. Why should people spend all their lives in jail? They should come out and be free. Of course they should go in for some time, I mean, they must pay for what they did, but not too long. Maybe a year or two.*

Check in the Key if you are not certain of your answers.

What to avoid (2)

There are two more things to avoid in your semi-formal style. One is artificial emphasis and the other is sloppy wording.

Artificial emphasis

A very general rule is:

   Good semi-formal writing does not need artificial emphasis.

Here are several sorts of artificial emphasis:

I have <u>NEVER</u> seen such an ugly cat! ! ! ! It MUST belong to Sara . . .

<u>Underlining</u>	Exclamation marks!!!!!!!
.....Rows of dots.....	
CAPITAL LETTERS	

All these are all right in informal writing – although even then they can be used too much. In semi-formal writing you should almost never use them.

You have to make your emphases in some other way. You have to explain yourself: that is, you have to *be explicit*. Your reader will not know what you mean with your dots and underlinings. What really lies behind those exclamation marks about the cat? *Show* what you mean – like this:

> *I had never in my life seen such an ugly cat: bald, obese, its fur dirty, its eyes half shut. The more I thought about it, the more I was convinced that it must belong to Sara. It was her sort of cat: pathetic, ferocious, unlovable.*

This is more work for the writer, but we are beginning to get some idea of what s/he really wants to say – without artifical emphasis.

Sloppy wording

'Wording' is the way you write something, the words you choose. 'Sloppy' means careless, thoughtless. Literally it means 'too loose' and is the result of not thinking about the details.

TASK 3

Below are some examples. What is sloppy about the wording? Think about them (discuss them if possible) and write your decision on each one.

N.B.   *You must do this before you look at the answers: it is essential that you yourself can see the fault before you are told what it is.*

1   I can't rely on her because she is so unreliable.

_____

2   She has never told me any lies, and when she did, she blushed.

_____

3   I think that prisoners today have too many privileges.

_____

4   Nowadays there is a high percentage of terrorism and consequently of crime.

_____

5   This is the tip of an iceberg which is going to break out again.

_____

Identify what is wrong in each case.

Now compare your answers with our comments.

1   This is a wonderful example of ***tautology***, i.e. saying the same thing twice. If you can't rely on her she **must** be unreliable. It is also a case of circular logic – like this conversation reported by an anthropologist:

Why do you do this?
   Because it is good.
How do you know it is good?
   Because our ancestors told us to do it.
Why did your ancestors tell you to do it?
   Because it is good.

2   This is a nice ***internal contradiction***. If she never told any lies, how could she blush when she did? This is a contradiction in terms, like saying 'my eight-year-old grandmother'.

3   This is a good case of ***overgeneralization***, a very common fault. The writer is in fact thinking about one small group of prisoners, but she seems to be speaking about them all. It is nonsense to imply that *all* prisoners today have a lot of privileges.

4   This is just generally ***loose wording***. Does 'a high percentage of terrorism' mean 'a lot of terrorism'? Moreover, terrorism is a crime, so crime cannot be a consequence of terrorism. The writer is not thinking.

5   This is a lovely ***mixed metaphor***. Icebergs don't usually *break out*.

TASK 4

Use the names above (tautology, etc.) to identify the problem.
Then rewrite the sentence, tightening up the wording.

1   In this Centre drug addicts are helped to stop doping themselves by renouncing drugs forever.

Problem   _____

Improvement _____
                _____

2   Unlike ordinary people, a model doesn't have a humdrum life; she often changes her husband or boyfriend.

Problem   _____

Improvement _____
                _____

3   Robinson Crusoe landed on a desert island inhabited only by savages.

Problem   _____

Improvement _____
                _____

4   We often think that a glamorous career is one of the best jobs which every one of us would like to have.

Problem   _____

Improvement _____
                _____

5 In this company we keep the door open for anyone who wants to rise to a higher position.

Problem   _____

Improvement _____

_____

6 I know he tells lies, because he is dishonest.

Problem   _____

Improvement _____

_____

7 The key to the problem is in our empty pockets.

Problem   _____

Improvement _____

_____

8 Young people these days spend all their lives looking for jobs and they never find them.

Problem   _____

Improvement _____

_____

Reading

Jargon and slang

Jargon, slang, 'bureaucratese', colloquialisms, swearing – you have a bit of everything in the selection at the end of this unit. Use them to discover your personal prejudices.

● What impression do you think people are trying to make in the flow diagram and the *Golden Bull Winner*?
● What do you think of them?
● Do you like the Australian slang? Would you use it if you lived in Australia?
● What is the flow-diagram about?
● Do you agree with:
   a Professor Taylor?
   b The Plain English Campaign, which selected the Golden Bull winner as a prime example of obscure official prose?

ASSIGNMENT 7

LANGUAGE

... My car's Cactus!

What aspects of language (your own or others) do you think should be encouraged or discouraged? What annoys you, or pleases you, about the way people speak and write, and the words they use?

Feedback work

Before you start your next assignment, do some feedback work on the previous one.

Planning

- You may know what you want to say, but rack your brain for good examples. Think about *accent*, *dialect*, *jargon*, *slang*, *style*, *'loanwords'* (borrowed from other languages), and about the way people speak – the people you know, people on television, bureaucrats and politicians, books, newspapers, etc.

- Select what you want to concentrate on – whatever interests *you*. You need to avoid just writing a list, so decide:
  - how your observations will hang together
  - what they are going to build up to at the end.

- Here are some possible overall structures:
  - what you like, and why, then what you dislike and why
  - everything you dislike, with the worst at the end
  - one tendency you have observed, with a lot of examples and a comment at the end
  - one practice you dislike, and what you would like to do about it.

FEEDBACK

To the reader

Please complete this checklist.

	YES/NO
Does the composition observe the document presentation requirements?	
Is it properly paragraphed?	
Can you identify the idea in each paragraph?	
Is the style not too elaborate and not too colloquial?	
Is there any sloppy wording?	
Select one good illustration/example.	
Do you agree with the writer? Please comment.	

DIARY PROMPT

Foreigners – the ones you see in films, the ones you see in the street, the ones you know. What do you know about them? How are they different from you? How do you feel about them? Make a list and choose one or two to write about.

Jargon and slang

Migrants to start profanity course

Teaching swearing to migrants is a new course being offered by an associate professor at the University of Sydney. Professor Brian Taylor, who has clocked up 20 years of research on bad language, started the course in order to help Australia's large migrant community to integrate into the local culture.

He said, "Swearing is so widespread now that migrants cannot avoid hearing it so they ought to know what it is all about."

He said that foreigners often got into trouble with the police because they did not understand what constituted offensive language. He also felt that students should be able to recognise when they were being abused and taught to respond accordingly.

Professor Taylor said that whilst swearing was becoming more widespread in Australia, the actual words used were uncreative. "We tend to use the same words over and over again without much imagination." he said. "The Australian Dictionary of Colloquialisms lists 'bloody' as 'the great Australian adjective'."

Golden Bull Winner

"There is an unavoidable conflict of terminology in naming the classes Class and Instantiation. Instantiation is not itself a real instance but a class (namely, the class of all real instances). Likewise Class is not a class of real instances but a class of classes (namely, the class of all classes of real instances). Instantiation could be renamed Class and Class renamed Type to avoid this. In that case the members of Class would not be classes and the members of Type would not be types."

STC Technology Ltd., Staffs;
Golden Bull Winner, 1989

A taste of Australian slang

Al Capone	– rhyming slang for a telephone
bottler	– a term used to express delight with someone – 'You little bottler!'
cactus	– totally useless – 'My car's cactus.'
drongo, droob	– a slow, pathetic, stupid person
Chrissie	– Christmas
face fungus	– a beard or moustache
idiot box	– the television
mystery bag	– a sausage
oldies	– parents
rellie	– a relative – 'I'm expecting all the rellies and oldies for Chrissie.'
rug rat	– a small child, a toddler
a sheila	– a woman
a sickie	– a day taken off work because of illness
a smoko	– time taken off work for a cigarette
up a gum tree	– in a hopeless situation
Woop Woop	– the most remote areas of the country – 'He comes from the back of Woop Woop.'

HOW MANY IT TAKES

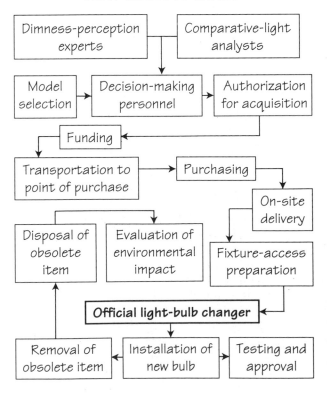

8 Language Preparation

! Look at Tests A and B for Unit 8, pages 151 and 153.

Contrasts

The only problem with making contrasts is knowing the right words to use. A little translation may help you to fix the appropriate equivalents.

Apart from *but*, the words normally used in English to make contrasts are:

while	although	by contrast	however
whereas	though	on the other hand	

Notice the distinction between **simple differences** and **contrasts in expectations**.

Simple differences

*Stan is small and thin, **while** Olly is big and fat.*

*Stan is small and thin, **whereas** Olly is big and fat.*

*Stan is small and thin. Olly, **by contrast**, is big and fat.*

*Stan is small and thin. Olly, **on the other hand**, is big and fat.*

Contrasts in expectations

***Although** Tom is always chasing Jerry, he never catches him.*

***Though** Tom is always chasing Jerry, he never catches him.*

*Tom is always chasing Jerry. He never catches him, **however**.*

*Tom is always chasing Jerry. He never catches him, **though**.*

Now ask yourself three questions

1   Which of these do you use and which ones do you not use?
2   What *other* expressions do you use instead?
3   What are the equivalents in your own language?

Discuss your answers with an expert if possible.

Link the parallel lives below with *while, whereas, on the other hand* or *by contrast*, as in the example. Then finish the story on both sides.

RAGS AND RICHES

The world was stunned when they announced their engagement.

She was born in a mansion in the Home Counties.	**while**	He was born in the back streets of Brooklyn.
Her father was a millionaire and her mother was an heiress.		His father was a petty gangster and his mother was a cleaner.

She had the best education money could buy.	He left school at fourteen.
She went to Oxford and got a degree in Law.	He joined a street gang selling drugs.

Add more contrasting sentences about:
ambitions   social life   achievements   hobbies

3 Make as many contrasting connections as you can between the **A** sentences and the **B** sentences, using *although*, *though* (in either position) and *however*.

A	B
They ate a lot of vitamins.	They both caught colds.
They started jogging to work.	They didn't feel any better.
They ate less animal fat.	Their cholesterol level went up.
They cut down on calories.	They didn't lose any weight.

Biodata

Birth, marriage and death – you can't get away from them, so you might as well get the language right!
  Here is the sad story. From birth to death, we move between **actions/events** and **states**.

Actions/events			**States**
Birth	We are born.	→	(We are alive!)
Marriage	We get married (*to* someone).	→	We are married (*to* someone).
	But sometimes		
Divorce	We get divorced (*from* someone).	→	We are divorced (*from* someone).
	And, finally		
Death	We die.	→	We are dead.

Now go back and check *each word*. What points do you need to learn (e.g. prepositions *to* and *from*, constructions with *get* and *are*, the form of the words)?

4 Fill in the gaps – rapidly.

a I was married [1]_____ an Englishman. I've no intention of [2]_____ married again. Why [3]_____ married when you're bound to [4]_____ divorced? All my friends [5]_____ divorced.

b Hemingway was [1]_____ in 1898 and [2]_____ in 1961. I was [3]_____ in 1970 and I'm not [4]_____ yet. This gives me at least one advantage over Hemingway.

c   I'm dying to get _____, but no-one will have me.

d   ¹_____ as a doornail, ²_____ as a dodo, ³_____ as
   mutton – which is the most ⁴_____ ?

▽ 5   Take your pick of the activities below. Write or speak, concentrating on giving
   the biodata correctly.

a   Describe your own marital situation very clearly – what it is, what is has
   been, what it might be, when and why.
b   Discuss the divorce laws in your country. What is the practice? Is it
   changing?
c   Give a very rapid mini-biography of any famous (dead) person: birth,
   marriage (happy/unhappy?), death.

Prepositions

Revise previous errors.

▽ 6   a   My flight was to Athens, but my luggage ended _____ in Rome.

b   He has a wonderful way of dealing _____ interruptions.

c   I have a great longing ___ ___ a really good ice-cream.

d   Health is something you should think _____ .

e   Salaries have not matched the rise _____ the cost of living.

f   He's married _____ a hairdresser, but he's completely bald. What a waste.

g   _____ the whole, I think I prefer the town to the country.

h   _____ chance I just happened to see what she had written.

i   There has been a huge improvement _____ your writing.

j   I'm not so keen _____ old movies as I used to be.

Check in the Key and rub out your mistakes.

▽ 7   Look in the previous preposition exercises for all the prepositions which go with
   changes (there are five). What conclusion can you draw?

Punctuation

There are two small important points on the punctuation of quotations.
1   First, these "......" and these '......' are English quotation marks. They are
   not like this:
   «Tomorrow, and tomorrow, and tomorrow»
   or like this: "Creeps in this petty pace from day to day„
   Instead, they are like this: "To the last syllable of recorded time".

2   You do not need to put quotation marks around ordinary words used with
   their normal meaning. For example, these are completely unnecessary:

My friends brought the 'dinner' with them: spaghetti with tomato sauce, cold meat and salad.

The dinner *was* a dinner: you don't need quotation marks.

Identify three of the famous quotations below, then put them in explanatory sentences, using conventional English punctuation.

Example   *To be or not to be.*

Hamlet said "To be or not to be" when he was thinking of suicide.

a   Eureka!
b   I have a dream
c   In the beginning was the Word
d   Out, damned spot!
e   I think, therefore I am
f   The wine-dark sea
g   She loves me, yeah, yeah, yeah
h   Carpe diem
i   I can resist everything except temptation
j   Life, liberty and the pursuit of happiness

1 _____

2 _____

3 _____

Get your sentences checked by an expert. You will find the origin of the quotations in the Key.

8 PINNING IT DOWN

Writing Tutorial

Examples and illustrations

We have already suggested that you should give examples and illustrations when you make a point in writing. In fact:

most of a composition is examples and illustrations.

The 'composition' of most compositions is:

IDEA (10%)	ILLUSTRATIONS ——————— EVIDENCE
	SUPPORT ———————(90%)——— EXAMPLES

You use your experience and knowledge to illustrate your ideas. We call it 'pinning down' ideas – bringing them into touch with reality.

Here is an example of a composition with no illustrations, no pinning down. Read it carefully, and also the reader's comments.

ON VICES AND VIRTUES

— What faults ? (a)

I know I have a lot of faults, which I must

try to cure. Sometimes I make big efforts, but

the trouble is, most of the time I'm too lazy.

— How ? (b)

It's not so easy to change yourself.

Also it's not so easy to see your own vices.

Sometimes you get a big shock when people

What do they say ? (c) —— criticize you. It's much easier to see other

people's faults and criticize them – and I must

say it's also more enjoyable.

Who ? (d) ——

However someone once told me that the faults

you see in other people are always your own

For example ? (e)

faults. I wonder if this can be true.

If so, I'd better improve myself quickly or

I really will not love myself any more!

This composition has a lot of good points. It has something to say, the English is all right, it has a nice shape, clearly reflected in the paragraphs. But it is pallid, it lacks impact. It needs *pinning down*.

Suppose this composition had been written by Dracula. Look at the beginning again:

'I know I have a lot of faults, which I must try to cure . . .'

Would you not agree that the writer has left out all the interesting information? And even if the writer is not Dracula, even if he is only one of us, we still want to know:
– what are his faults?
– what did he try to do about them?
– what did people say to him when they criticized him? Why was it such a shock?

TASK 1

Look at the reader's comments. What are they asking for: examples, illustrations, quotations, details/particulars?

a _____

b _____

c _____

d _____

e _____

Check in the Key if you are not sure.

E-QU-I-P

These are all ways of pinning the subject down.

| E - xamples |
| QU - otations | E-QU-I-P
| I - llustrations |
| P - articulars |

You use all these already. What you need to do is use them *more*.

1 Examples

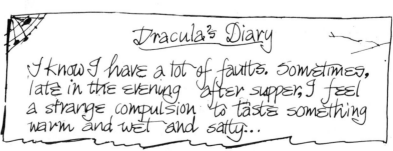

Concrete examples almost always make your writing more interesting and convincing.

Idea The restaurant was not very clean.

Idea plus examples The restaurant was not very clean. The glasses had watermarks on them and on my knife there was something which looked like dried blood but was probably old tomato sauce.

TASK
2

Below are some more examples. Underline only the parts which are *examples*.

1   Many stars had difficulties at the beginning of their careers. Michelle Pfeiffer, for example, began by shooting TV commercials and when she entered films was immediately typecast as the dumb blonde and could not get any other kind of part.

2   Military service is obviously of some use to those who benefit from it economically (arms and equipment manufacturers and dealers, builders, ministry employees, career officers and so on). But military service was presumably not intended to be simply an employment programme.

3   Is American culture taking over the world? *McDonald's* has arrived in Moscow, we all watch *Dallas*, *Coca-Cola* is replacing wine and beer and everybody smokes *Marlboro*. At the same time many languages have been influenced by American English and the word 'OK' is universal.

4   As for washing dishes and cleaning toilets, cooking and 'becoming a man', I think these are not the business of the state and military service, but of parents, schools and the person himself.

Check in the Key if you are not sure about your answers.

2   Quotations

When you write about someone saying something, ask yourself: 'Why not use a quotation?'. Quotations can add conviction and interest and liveliness to a composition. For example, you can use a quotation from real life:

> My mother is a real tyrant. She is always telling us what to do. 'Take off your shoes, Angela!' 'Bob, don't play your cassettes so loud!'

Or you may be able to use a quotation from a book or a newspaper or the television.

> *I saw in the newspaper last Tuesday the headline 'The right to die?'. It was about a girl who had been kept alive in hospital by a machine for seven years.*

You can also of course use famous quotations.

> *When Armstrong landed on the moon, he said 'One small step for man, one gigantic step for mankind' (or words to that effect). But to my mind mankind hasn't really taken any big steps forward this century, not even in space exploration.*

3   Illustrations

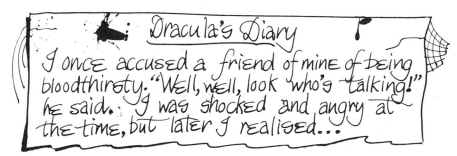

Illustrations are much the same as examples, but often longer. They are 'illustrations' because they 'show' – vividly – what the writer is talking about. Here is the beginning of a composition which desperately needs illustrating:

> *People talk a lot about violence on TV and indeed there is a lot of violence of different kinds, sometimes in fiction films and sometimes real violence shown on the news.*

TASK 3

1   Think how you would illustrate this idea. Search your own experience for some evidence to support it.

2   Write a sentence or two below, making sure they really illustrate what the writer wants to say.

3   Use an arrow ⟵ to show where you would insert your illustration in the composition.

_____

_____

_____

_____

 Do not continue until you have done this exercise.

The writer of this composition eventually rewrote the beginning like this:

> *People talk about violence on television and indeed a lot of violence of different kinds is shown. I once saw a film in which a man was shot; his blood splashed over the lens of the camera so that we saw it run down the TV screen. The effect was shocking. But violence is not only to be seen in fiction films; the news, too, constantly shows us scenes of real violence. Just recently I saw ...*

You can see how much more powerful the idea is when it is illustrated.

Illustrations don't just support ideas, they also change and improve them. Ideas need illustrating. So get some practice thinking of illustrations.

TASK 4

Below are some very general points. Try to find material – true material from your personal experience – to illustrate them. Write just one illustration after each general point.

1   Bureaucracy can be very frustrating. _____

_____

2   Most television programmes are rubbish, 'chewing-gum for the eyes'. _____

_____

3   Good writing can to some extent be learnt. _____

_____

4   It is sometimes very difficult to avoid breaking the law. _____

_____

5   I am sure that boys are psychologically different from girls. _____

_____

4   Particulars

Dracula's Diary
My aunt Pipistrella
~~Someone~~ once told me that
a vampire's life is never easy...

A standard technique of professional writers is to 'particularize' – that is, always to give concrete details instead of vague generalities. Here are two examples:

Vague and general ▼ He has tried *all sorts of jobs* but he gave them all up.

More specific ▼ He has tried *being a waiter, a barman, a rubbish collector and a messenger*, but he gave them all up.

Vague and general   She takes her holidays in *glamorous places*.

▼   ▼

More specific   She takes her holidays in *Florida, Acapulco, Tibet*, always somewhere glamorous.

Look for this technique in novels. You will see that they don't usually say 'He started eating', but 'He picked up the bread and bit into it' or 'He started cutting up the steak' or 'He spooned in the soup noisily'. Details and particulars like this make it easier for the reader to visualize – more readable, in fact.

TASK 5

Particularizing is an easy technique to learn. It is also good for your vocabulary. Get your dictionary and make the sentences below more particular, more specific, more interesting by changing the italicized words.

1   Every evening she waters *the flowers* on her balcony.

_____

2   She always wears *beautiful expensive clothes*.

_____

3   He steals *little things* from shops.

_____

4   The car was dirty and full of *rubbish*.

_____

5   He wastes his money on *silly things*.

_____

6   When you do military service, you have to *do a lot of domestic tasks*.

_____

 Consult the Key for further ideas.

TASK 6

Below is the outline of a composition. We have given you only the ideas which constituted the frame of the composition – all the examples, illustrations and details have been left out.

How would you illustrate these ideas – from your own experience, observation and knowledge? Think of all possible sources – family, friends, films, books, songs, etc.

1   Until recently, women were not free.   _____

_____

2   Now they can legally do everything men can do.   _____

_____

3   But this 'freedom' is still not completely real.   _____

_____

4   Women must make this freedom a reality.   _____

_____

TASK

Now read the original composition and compare your ideas with it.

Are women liberated enough – or too much?

On Thursday evening I watched a film on TV called 'The Colour Purple'. It was the story of a black woman who was not free: when she was young she was sold as wife to a man who regarded her as a slave and she never tried to rebel.

Nowadays I cannot say that women are still slaves in this way. They can study, vote, work and, most important of all, they can choose. Not so long ago, in many places the birth of a girl was a disgrace: she was only another girl to marry off. Nowadays, being a woman is not a disgrace.

However, I think that women only appear to be free. There are few women managers and usually their jobs are connected to the 'woman's world' (fashion, cosmetics, women's magazines, etc.). On TV, for example, there are not many women journalists and they often owe their jobs to their beautiful faces, not to their heads – despite the fact that, according to an opinion poll, many audiences (for example Italians) actually prefer women on TV.

It is no longer enough to regard the women's world as a bad photocopy of the men's. The big battle of this century is, I think, to make the apparent freedom a reality: women must discover their own full identity. There are some initiatives towards this. I have read that a number of centres have been set up where women can speak about their problems, can find friends and get support in their troubles.

Naturally I do not want to go to the other extreme. I hope that the society of males and females will be an equal world. It's unrealistic to think that women can become the centre of the world and men simply satellites. But we still have some way to go towards a better balance.

Now read the composition again, more analytically.
1   Which paragraphs deal with each main idea?
2   How does the writer illustrate each main idea?
3   Which illustration do you think has most force?

Check in the Key and compare your answers.

Reading

The hurled ashtray

Nora Ephron is a columnist – that is to say, she is one of the few people who are actually paid to write just what *they* want to write. She has a chatty colloquial style (which you may imitate only when you are as good as she is). One thing she understands is the art of illustration: her articles are packed with anecdotes and all of them make a point.

You will find her article, *The Hurled Ashtray*, at the end of this unit. This article was clearly the outcome of some intense discussion in Nora Ephron's social circle, so the best thing you can do with this extract is to ask yourselves the same question that Nora asked her friends, and go on from there.

We hope you have heard of Gary Cooper, famous star of the silver screen. You may not have heard of Teddy Boys, the wild young men of the time.

A few of the key words are: *swell* (American English), *misbehaving, threatening, cowed, sniggering, leering, a looker* (American English), *appendages*. It will help if you find out what they mean before you start.

ASSIGNMENT 8

Below is an advertisement for a competition run by an English language teaching magazine. We suggest you enter for it by writing the composition.

A woman's place . . .

Woman to woman, the English language teaching magazine written specially for women learners of English, is holding a competition for listeners to win a place at an English language Summer School.

The prize is a place on a three-week general language course, which includes conversation, role-play, discussion, debate and project work as well as seminars and language lab sessions.

Listeners who want to enter the competition must write, in no more than 300 words, an account of what they think life is like for women in their country.

Feedback work

Before you do your next assignment, do some feedback work on the last one.

Planning: illustrations and examples

As you make your notes, try using two different coloured pens to distinguish between points which are clearly *ideas* and those which are clearly *illustrations* or *examples*. This way you can see if some ideas still need pinning down.

When you have developed and organized your ideas, write down the frame of your composition – the three or four main points in sequence – like the example on page 116. This will also help you to see what needs illustration.

The subjects of your compositions are getting less personal, but this does not mean you should neglect your own experience. To illustrate this composition, go back to what you yourself think and feel and have seen and read – and do not start writing until you have something which you really want to say.

FEEDBACK

To the reader

Please complete this questionnaire.

	YES/NO
Are all the document presentation requirements fulfilled?	
Is the composition properly paragraphed, i.e. do the physical paragraphs reflect separate ideas?	
How many illustrations and examples can you identify in the composition?	
Which is the best one, in your opinion?	
Do you agree with what the writer says about women? Please comment.	
Please make one suggestion for improvement.	

DIARY PROMPT

The subject is *Superstition*, which is not just ghosts and apparitions and horoscopes, but also blue clothes for baby boys, mascots at football matches, wishing on a chicken bone, hanging up horseshoes and not walking on the cracks in the pavement.

Do you think (sincerely) that you are not superstitious? If so, what do you think of people who are? Do you think superstition is harmless or dangerous? If you are superstitious, what do you do for luck – or to prevent bad luck? Do you ever act on what the cards, or the zodiac, or your dreams tell you? Have there been any events in your life that seemed 'meant to happen'? Tell all.

THE HURLED ASHTRAY

I once heard a swell story about Gary Cooper... The story was that Gary Cooper was in a London restaurant at a large table of friends. He was sitting in a low chair, with his back to the rest of the room, so no one in the restaurant even knew that he was tall, much less that he was Gary Cooper. Across the way was a group of Teddy Boys (this episode took place long long ago, you see), and they were all misbehaving and making nasty remarks about a woman at Cooper's table. Cooper turned around to give them his best threatening stare, but they went right on. Finally he got up, very very slowly, so slowly that it took almost a minute for him to go from this short person in a low chair to a ten-foot-tall man with Gary Cooper's head on top of his shoulders. He loped over to the table of Teddy Boys, looked down at them, and said 'Wouldja mind sayin' that agin?' The men were utterly cowed and left the restaurant shortly thereafter.

I thought of Gary Cooper and his way with words the other day. Longingly. Because in the mail came an excerpt from a book by Michael Korda which made a fascinating, though pathetic, contrast to the Gary Cooper story. It seems that Korda, his wife and another woman were having dinner in a London restaurant. Across the way was a table of drunks, sniggering and leering and throwing bread balls at Mrs Korda, who is a looker. Her back was to them, and she refused to acknowledge their presence. Then, one of the men sent over a waiter with a silver tray. On it was a printed card, the kind you can buy in novelty shops, which read: 'I want to sleep with you! Tick off your favorite love position from the list below, and return this card with your telephone number ...'. Korda tore up the card before his wife could even see it, and then, consumed with rage, he picked up an ashtray and threw it at the man who had sent the card. A fracas ensued, and before long, Korda, his wife, and their woman friend were out on the street. Mrs Korda was furious.

'If you ever do that again,' she screamed, 'I'll leave you! Do you think I couldn't have handled that, or ignored it? Did I ask you to come to my defense against some poor stupid drunk? You didn't even think, you just reacted like a male chauvinist. You leapt up to defend *your* woman, *your* honor, you made me seem cheap and foolish and powerless ... can't you see it was none of your business! Can't you understand how it makes me feel? It's really sickening ... it's like being a slave!' Korda concludes that his wife is doubtless right, that men do tend to treat women merely as appendages of themselves.

The magazine *New York* asked several couples, including my husband and me, what our reaction was to the story and what we would have done under the circumstances. My first reaction to the entire business was that no one ever sends me notes like that in restaurants. My second was that it was absurd for Mrs Korda to think that she alone was involved in the incident. Yes, it might have been nice if her husband had consulted her; and yes, it would have been even nicer if he had been Gary Cooper. But the fact remains that the men at the table *were* insulting Korda and disturbing his dinner as well as hers. Their insult was childish and Korda's reaction was ludicrous, but Mrs Korda matched them all by reducing a complicated and rather interesting emotional situation to a tedious set of feminist platitudes.

I told the story over dinner to four friends and asked for their reaction. The first, a man, said that he thought Mrs Korda was completely right. The second, a woman, said she thought Korda's behavior was totally understandable. The third, a man, said that both parties had behaved badly. The fourth, my friend Martha, said it was the second most boring thing she had ever heard, the most boring being a story I had just told her about a fight my college roommate had with a cabdriver at Kennedy Airport...

9 Language Preparation

! Look at Tests A and B for Unit 9, pages 151 and 154.

The genitive or not?

When people have learned the English genitive, they often start to overuse it. For example, they say '**traffic's problems**' instead of '**traffic problems**' or '**the problems of traffic**'.

This is **not** a simple area of language. The best way to learn it is probably just through exposure, rather than studying a lot of rules. We only want to give you one guideline and help you to use it in case of need.

There are two special characteristics of the genitive:

1 It is generally used with people, animals, human organizations – something **animate**, e.g. *the dog's biscuits, women's ideas, our club's programme, Terry's behaviour, the government's proposals, the world's rivers.*

2 The first word **has** or **produces** the second word. That is, the dog *has* biscuits, women *have* ideas, our club *has* a programme, Terry *produces* behaviour, the government *produces* proposals, the world *has* rivers.

So if you are not sure whether to use the genitive, ask two questions:

1 Is the first word animate?
2 Does the first word have or produce the second word?

If they are both true you usually need the genitive.

Look through the examples below and make an *instinctive* choice in each case. Then go back and ask the two questions above. See if your instincts were right.

a I belong to *Capricorn's sign / the sign of Capricorn.*
b *Her teddy bear's foot / Her teddy bear foot* has fallen off.
c *The houses' windows / The windows of the houses* were all open.
d *Palestine's question / The question of Palestine* concerns many nations.
e *Scotland's position / The Scotland position* in the UK is getting stronger.
f *Our experts' team / Our team of experts* have made a different proposal.
g Parachuting enables you to experience *the flight's ecstasy / the ecstasy of flight.*
h *The finance's world / The world of finance* is in trouble.
i What are we doing to resolve *the pollution's problems / the problems of pollution?*
 j *Children's rights / Children rights* are only just beginning to be recognized.

Economics and politics

Like birth and death, *economics* and *politics* are always with us and the whole family of related words presents a lot of little difficulties.

2 Try to fill in this chart about the form of the words. Do it in pencil, then check in the Key and correct your answers.

		Economics	Politics
a	**The subjects** are	*economics*	*politics*
b	**The people** are	_____	_____
c	**The plans** they have are		_____
d	**The aspect of the country** is	the _____	the _____ system
e	**The adjectives** are	_____	_____
		_____	
f	**The adverbs** are	_____	_____

3 Now do this for reinforcement. When you have checked the answers, read the sentences aloud to get the word stress right.

a   Most of today's p _____ are men – why?

b   Russia's e _____ is in a mess, but there will have to be a

 p _____ solution before there is an e _____ one.

c   This car's very e _____ to run.

d   The drug trade should be seen as an e _____ problem with an

 e _____ solution.

e   There are too many e _____ at the World Bank; as a result the

 Banks's p _____ are too monetary.

f   Denis studied p _____ , philosophy and e _____

 at university, with a view to a career in p _____

g   It's a good p _____ for sportsmen to retire at the peak of their

 success, but they seldom do.

h   Protecting the environment is often not e _____ attractive in

 the short term, but is becoming p _____ very important.

Prepositions

Revise previous errors.

4

a   She does the shopping because she's clever _____ bargaining.

b   Do the exercise _____ pencil.

c   I stayed at home to look _____ my mother, who was sick.

d   I came to Liverpool _____ accident: I took the wrong train.

e   Apart _____ your relatives, who will you be seeing at Christmas?

f   I'm reasonably happy _____ the way this has been organized.

g   I suppose _____ some extent we could have done better.

h   Ask _____ the postman why your letters are so late.

i   _____ and large, the press is free, although there are some small restrictions.

j   England has a lot of wonderfully fattening food such _____ biscuits, cakes and sweets.

5   Look back at previous preposition exercises for:

–   adjectives for capacities and attitudes (there are six). What prepositions do you find?

–   expressions meaning *generally* (there are three).

Spelling

Irregular verbs in English are a headache, and in some cases the spelling is also rather strange.

6   a   See if you can remember the simple past forms of the verbs below.

bring _____	buy _____	catch _____
deal _____	fight _____	hear _____
mean _____	read _____	teach _____
think _____	win _____	

b   Then make sure you can pronounce them properly.

9 ORGANIZATION (1)

Writing Tutorial

In this part we are talking about: **shape, direction, relevance,** or **form**. It is a quality of writing which is highly prized in some parts of the world and not so valued in others. So what we want you to learn is to some extent a cultural thing. When you have learnt to do it, you can decide for yourself whether you want to go on doing it.

Do you need practice?

From your discussion with your teacher/tutor, you should know whether organization is one of your weak points. Most students (including most native speakers) need some improvement in this area.

About one student in ten has a real deep-seated problem with organization. Usually they know it. Such students are often very imaginative and have interesting thoughts and strong feelings: they just can't arrange them in order. Their writing is chaotic. If you are one of these, do not despair. You will have to work harder on this aspect of your writing, but you really can improve. And you have the great advantage that you always have something interesting to say.

What goes wrong

There are several main faults of form.

- **Weak beginnings** The composition starts in the middle.
- **Weak endings** The composition has no real ending.
- **Rambling writing** The thought is linear and lacks direction.
- **Confused writing** The points are not dealt with one by one but are all mixed up together.

We will look at the first three in this unit and at confused writing in the next unit.

Beginnings

Usually the beginning is the easy part. But sometimes writers rush into their compositions as if they were just continuing a conversation. This is fine if you know what they are talking about. If you don't, you are in the dark.

As an example, here's the beginning of a composition (it had no title). As you read, try to answer these questions: Who is Vitelli? What are they doing with him? Why is it good?

> *I think that what they are doing with Vitelli is quite good although it needs more control. Indeed, jail has to be a place for developing better citizens and not better criminals.*

TASK 1

Do we know what this writer is talking about? No. The writer has not taken time to explain. We have to work it out for ourselves.

Filling in the reader

When you write a composition you have to assume:
   a   that you have a lot of readers, and
   b   that most of them do not know what you are talking about.
You have to give them all the information they need to understand what you are saying. We call this 'filling the readers in' or 'filling in the background', or 'putting the readers in the picture'. It is an important part of reader-awareness, which is an important part of being a good writer.

Here is the same composition, with the beginning rewritten. This time it fills the readers in very well.

> *In the 1960s and 1970s there was a terrible period of political terrorism in Italy. You may remember some of the most shocking actions, for example, the kidnapping and killing of Aldo Moro and the bombing of Bologna railway station.*
>
> *Some of the terrorists died, some disappeared and some were caught and put in prison. One of these was Roberto Vitelli ...*

Now we know where we are. The writer has put us in the picture.

Endings

More frequently, the composition doesn't have a proper ending. You can't think of anything more to say, so you just stop. A good ending relates to the *whole* of the composition. A weak ending usually relates only to the last part. Here is an example. The writer is talking about virtues and vices, mostly those of her sister.

First she describes her sister's awful habit of smoking at the table.

Then she says that her sister is nevertheless a very sincere girl and that she and her sister tell each other a lot of secrets.

Then she talks about her sister's even worse habit of breaking promises.

Ending ?

TASK 2

Here are three endings for this composition. Which do you think would fit best? You are looking for one which relates to the **whole of the composition**.

Ending 1   Sincerity is important in family life because it strengthens family relationships.

Ending 2   Sincerity is important in family life because it strengthens family relationships. But I think sincerity is only a beginning. There must be consideration and trust as well.

Ending 3 Sincerity is important in family life because it strengthens family relationships. But even more important is love.

 Check in the Key if you are not sure about your answer.

You should see that one of the endings simply continues the subject, one introduces a new subject, and one deals with the whole subject of the composition and brings it to a conclusion.

A good ending should 'wrap up' the subject, as you wrap up a parcel: it should make the reader feel that this is 'The End', not the middle or a new beginning.

How to end

We can't tell you how to end your composition. It depends on what you have to say. As we have said before, one way to get a good ending is to think how to end *before* you start writing: always keep the best to the last. Alternatively, we can give you a very boring way of ending which you can use if you can't think of anything else.

1 Start a new paragraph.
2 Write *In conclusion* or *To conclude* or *To sum up* or *In short*.
3 Then repeat everything you have said before, but in summary form.
4 Stop.

This is a last resort. But it is better than no ending at all.

TASK 3 Below and on the next page is a composition about being a model. We have removed the ending – it took up three lines.
1 Read the composition through and try to think of a good ending, one which wraps up the subject.
2 If you can't think of a good ending, write a 'last resort' ending instead.
3 Then compare your ending with the original one.

 Check in the Key for the original ending.

Possible ending (last paragraph)

> A modelling career is a wonderful dream for most people. It can make you rich and famous, your face becomes familiar to the whole world. A model is always well-dressed and made up and always has beautifully done hair. She knows a lot of countries because she travels everywhere by private plane. She meets other interesting and famous people.
>
> Becoming a model is difficult because you have to have particular qualities; for example, you must be quite tall, thin and pretty.
>
> Models usually live in comfortable flats and they do not have to do boring things like cooking or cleaning their houses; they usually have a personal maid to do these things for them.

> *Things change when we look at a model's life more closely. In reality, working as a model means a lot of sacrifices, like being always on a diet, having very little time for private life and also working when you are sick.*
>
> *But the worst thing is that a model has a very short-term career. When she gets old she is replaced by younger women and is forgotten and neglected. She continues her life as a normal person, but (I imagine) with lots of regrets.*

_____

_____

_____

Rambling

This is rambling. Rambling is perfectly natural. Your mind rambles when it is not focusing on one thing in particular. It is like a car when it is not in gear.

Rambling can be quite interesting. It is sometimes used in novels to show how someone's mind works when it is running freely, without control, moving from subject to subject at random.

But rambling is something we do not want in a composition. It means that the writer doesn't know where he's going, has no direction, has no *reason* for writing. Rambling results in 'linear' writing, where one sentence suggests the next sentence, which suggests the next sentence, and so on.

Here is an example:

> *I was born in a little village called Stowton. In fact Stowton is not a very exciting place to live, as my friend Mac often points out. He used to work there as a carpenter, but he left when he got married to Julia and went to live near to Julia's family. They are quite rich (lucky Mac!). They have a factory which makes biscuits. The biscuits are famous and they export a lot. In fact I bought some when I was in France.*

TASK 4

Look at how the subject changes. The first sentence is about 'I'. What about the others?

Sentence	Subject
Example 2	*Stowton*
3	_____

4 _____

5 _____

6–7 _____

 Check in the Key if you need to.

The last subject is a very long way from the first. This is because rambling writing comes from not knowing what you want to say. This writer has no idea where he is going, he can't stick to the point, he has 'lost the thread'. Perhaps he never had a thread to start with.

TASK 5

See if you can recognize a 'thread' easily and quickly. Starting with the first sentence below, pick out the line (A, B or C) which 'follows the thread', (the others wander from the point).

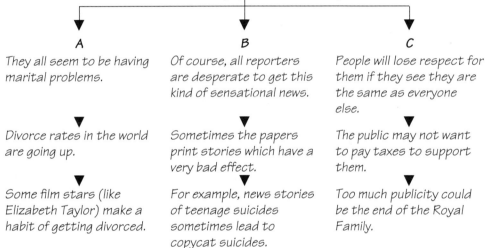

The Royal Family should keep quiet about their private affairs.

A
They all seem to be having marital problems.

Divorce rates in the world are going up.

Some film stars (like Elizabeth Taylor) make a habit of getting divorced.

B
Of course, all reporters are desperate to get this kind of sensational news.

Sometimes the papers print stories which have a very bad effect.

For example, news stories of teenage suicides sometimes lead to copycat suicides.

C
People will lose respect for them if they see they are the same as everyone else.

The public may not want to pay taxes to support them.

Too much publicity could be the end of the Royal Family.

 Check in the Key if you need to.

Prevention and cure

You can **prevent** rambling writing simply by having something to say and saying it. You cannot **cure** rambling writing once it has been written. You can only throw it away, find something you want to say and start again. But you can cure small digressions by checking your work after writing to see if you have wandered from the point.

TASK 6

1   Go back to the composition about being a model. It is quite well organized: the first part is about the glamorous image of the model and the second part is about the unglamorous reality. Only one small part does not fit – that is, it *digresses* from the main point. Find it.

2   Write the first three words and the last three words of the digression.

O—🗝   *Check in the Key if you are not sure.*

Reading

Testimony

One place where relevance and purpose are of supreme importance is in courtroom questioning. Good courtroom questioning is an excellent example of tight speaking for anyone who is learning tight writing. Questioning a witness is not so different from writing a composition. Both are trying to show something. Both have to keep to the point and avoid digressions. The writer leavers the best to last in order to make the point as strongly as possible; the lawyer keeps the message to the end because all the questioning is leading up to the point.

The transcript you have at the end of this unit is a little bit of history. It is the questioning of a black witness, who had made applications to register as a voter, in a civil rights case in Alabama in 1958: a significant case at a significant time. The quiet, prosaic tone of the questioning covers strong emotions and dramatic implications.

The very end of the dialogue reveals the *point* of the questioning. Before you look at the last two questions and answers, try to work out just what the lawyer is trying to do. What is the point he is leading up to?

How (and where, and why) does he change the rhythm of the questioning?

What is the purpose of each of his questions?

ASSIGNMENT 9

The subject is:

INJUSTICE

- *What is your experience of injustice?*
- *What conclusions can you draw from your experience?*

Feedback work

Do some feedback work on your last assignment before starting this composition.

Planning: avoiding hot air

- You are writing about wider subjects now. The danger is that you will say a lot of very general, very obvious things – a higher level of hot air – and lose touch with your own thoughts, feelings and experience.
- To avoid this, look for a real-life case, an anecdote which will symbolize your idea of what is unjust. Think of all areas of life and all kinds of injustice – personal, social, economic, legal. Do you have any feelings of indignation or resentment? They are probably inspired by an injustice.
- Start with the anecdote, then comment on it. Say why it happened, why you think it was wrong and how it could have been avoided. Try to make your reader feel the way you feel about it.
- Stick to the subject!

FEEDBACK

To the reader

Please complete this questionnaire.

	YES/NO
Does the composition fulfil all documentation presentation requirements?	
Is it properly paragraphed in both senses?	
Is it free of rambling and digressions?	
Is/Are the example(s) interesting?	
Is the style appropriate?	
If you had to rate this injustice on a scale of 1 to 5 (1 = not at all serious, 5 = very serious), where would you put it?	
Do you agree with the writer about the injustice s/he has described? Please comment.	
Any other comments (compliments, suggestions for improvement, thoughts on the language)?	

DIARY PROMPT

Think of a specific person you are in conflict with. Imagine that you have decided finally to 'have it out' with this person, to try and get your point of view across. Think realistically about what you would say, and what s/he would say. Then write the script of your conversation.

TESTIMONY

Testimony of William Andrew Hunter, Associate Professor of Education and Acting Dean, School of Education, Tuskegee Institute, Macon County, Alabama.

Q Please state your name, age, and place of birth.
A William Andrew Hunter, forty-five years of age, born in North Little Rock, Arkansas.
Q How long have you lived in Alabama?
5 A Since 1950. Eight years.
Q And where is your residence?
A In Macon County, Alabama.
Q How long have you lived there?
A Eight years. Since 1950.
10 Q Are you married?
A Yes.
Q What official position, if any, do you hold?
A In Macon County there is Tuskegee Institute. I am an Associate Professor of Education there and Acting Dean of Education in the School of Education.
15 Q How long have you held that position?
A About three years as associate professor: only two years as Acting Dean.
Q How long did you live in Arkansas?
A Until I was drafted into the service in 1942.
Q How long did you serve in the armed forces?
20 A Three years, three months.
Q What branch of the service?
A In the Finance Service, Army.
Q Are you a graduate of any high school?
A Yes, Dunbar High School, Little Rock, Arkansas.
25 Q Any degree?
A It's a teacher's certificate.
Q Have you been a teacher since that time?
A Since 1936, I have been a teacher.
Q All right, next?
30 A Then the Bachelor of Science, Wilberforce University, a degree in chemistry.
Q All right, next?
A I received the Master of Science degree in Science education and research from Iowa State College in 1948, and the Ph.D. degree from Iowa State College in science education, research and statistics in 1952.
35 Q Are you a member of any scholastic societies or professional societies?
A The Phi Beta Kappa, honorary society. I am a member of that. Beta Kappa Chi, honorary scientific society. The National Teacher's Association, the National Educational Association, to mention a few, YMCA, and such others.
Q Belong to any church?
40 A Yes. The Methodist Church.
Q Do you have any physical or mental disabilities?
A None.
Q Have you ever been arrested or convicted of any crime?

A   No, I have not.

45   Q   Did you ever make application to vote in Macon County?

A   Yes, I did.

Q   When?

A   My first application was made during 1954. Of course I made several others. . . .

Q   Just tell the commission what you did and the steps you took and what happened.

50   A   Well, on several occasions during January of 1954 I went to the Macon County courthouse and stood in line.

Q   Stood in line for what?

A   To register. This was the line that was lined up before the registration room.

Q   Did you get into the room the first day?

55   A   No, I did not.

Q   Well, why didn't you?

A   The line was too long.

Q   All right. Then when did you go back? How soon after that?

A   Oh, the next time the registrars convened. I can't exactly remember the time.

60   Q   Do you remember how many times you went through that before you got in?

A   About three times.

Q   After you got inside, just tell what happened.

A   I was given the application form which I filled out, and it must have taken me about two hours to do so.

65   Q   All right. What happened next?

A   I self-addressed an envelope and was told I would hear from the board if I passed. Of course, I didn't hear from the board. I waited six months before I tried again.

Q   And what did you do that time? Was it the same . . .

A   Same procedure.

70   Q   Did you hear from that application?

A   I have not heard from them yet.

Q   Was that the last time you made the application?

A   That was the last time.

Q   Then you made two?

75   A   Yes.

Q   And went through the similar procedure indicated?

A   That's right.

Q   Did you fill out all the forms that were required?

A   Yes, I did.

80   Q   How long were you in the room?

A   Approximately two hours.

Q   Did you write what they requested you to write?

A   Yes, I did.

Q   Did you answer all the questions?

85   A   Yes, I did.

Q   And you never heard from them since?

A   No, I haven't.

Q   You never received your registration?

A   No, I haven't.

90   Q   Do you know why you are not registered?

A   I think it was certainly because I am a Negro.

Q   Do you know of any other reason?

A   None that I can logically justify or reasonably understand.

10 Language Preparation

! Look at Tests A and B for Unit 10, pages 151 and 154.

Connections

There are many ways of talking about the connection between one thing and another. Some of them are:

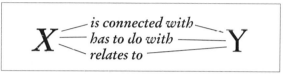

These are some ways of expressing closer connections:

$$X \overline{\quad\begin{array}{c}\textit{deals with}\\ \textit{is concerned with}\end{array}\quad} Y$$

We want to look at just one of these – probably the most common and useful one: **have to do with**. If you say that one thing *has to do with* another, you mean that the two things are connected in some way – any way.

1 To get the idea, just answer these questions.

  a What does petrol have to do with coal?
  b How much do you think happiness has to do with wealth?
  c What does a chicken have to do with a ball of string?
  d What does iron have to do with an iron?
  e What do Brazilian rainforests have to do with us?

 Check in the Key if necessary.

The connection can be strong or weak, very relevant or not very relevant. You can say, for example:

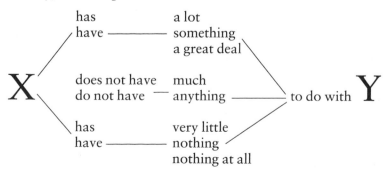

Choose the expression you think is right for the sentences below. (Your answers will be subjective and you may need to discuss them.)

a   Acid rain _____ nuclear power stations.

b   The increase in crime _____ drugs.

c   Beards _____ personality.

d   Giving up smoking _____ how rich you are.

e   Giving up smoking _____ will-power.

Opinions

Giving opinions is something that writers often do badly, but it is very easy to improve. You have to do three things:

1   Make sure it *is* an opinion, and not a fact. Don't write (for example) 'In my opinion, America is a very big country.' This is not an opinion.

2   Stop saying 'I think . . .' all the time. It's boring! Change it! Diversify!

3   Use genuine English opinion expressions and not your own inventions. Some acceptable expressions are below: check which ones you personally don't use (or don't use correctly) and add them to your repertoire.

	Use?			Use?
To my mind, ...		I don't feel that		
As I see it, ...		I don't agree that		
In my opinion, ...		I would not say that		

!   *You cannot say* **according to me, I am agree, by me.**

To give you practice in using these expressions, we give you some statements below to agree with, disagree with, or (best of all) qualify, according to your own opinion. Write your responses first, then (if possible) use them to start a discussion. Begin with 'Yes', 'No' or 'Well . . .' and underline the words you use to show that you are giving your opinion. The first one is done as an example.

a   For man, a *femme fatale* is more attractive than an ordinary woman because a *femme fatale* is safe: she doesn't want to marry him or pursue him.

> *Well, yes, but* **I would say that** *the main attraction of a femme fatale is the mystery. Because she does not reveal herself, it is possible to project fantasies on her.*

b   Some people think they don't believe in astrology, but deep down everyone is superstitious. And this is a good argument for a belief in astrology.

c Dogs are more generous, more lovable, more loving and more loyal than cats – in short, they are simply nicer.

_____

d You can never get rid of corruption in politics: you can only hide it (and some countries are more successful at hiding it than others). Power and corruption go hand in hand.

_____

_____

e They said God is dead – but there are many different Gods. There's God the creator, God the moral judge, God the old man in heaven and God the personal friend. Some are less dead than others.

_____

_____

f The pop/rock music market is completely cynical, concerned only with manufacturing and selling.

_____

_____

Prepositions

Revise previous errors.

4

a Take care _____ the pence and the pounds will take care _____ themselves.

b _____ my opinion, they've gone too far this time.

c I am convinced he did it _____ purpose.

d That's what they say – but I'd like to see it _____ writing.

e It's completely irrelevant – it has nothing to do _____ it.

f _____ my mind, the worst part of air travel is waiting around at the airport.

g The adults can look after themselves. _____ regards the children, we'd better organize some kind of party.

h I have the impression that the lake has decreased _____ size.

i I agree _____ your proposal in principle.

j _____ regard to the gas cooker, we hardly use it.

5

Look through previous preposition exercises for:

– ways of expressing intention, or lack of it (there are three). What are the prepositions?

– verbs involving responsibility (there are four). Do they all have the same preposition?

Punctuation

The exercise below deals with punctuating the genitive, which you looked at in the last unit. The purpose of the exercise is diagnostic – to find out if there are any points you are not sure of.

Put in apostrophes (') where you think they are necessary.

Can you evaluate a schools performance by its examination results? This is the interesting question raised by the British Governments decision to publish schools examination results and rank the schools in a 'league table'. There was a furious reaction from some schools. Mrs Jaggers, headmistress of Subeaton Comprehensive School, said, 'The government is out of touch. It is quite clear that their priorities are not the same as ours. Results depend on the areas the schools are in and on the local councils policies as much as on each schools efforts'. Mrs Jaggers schools results are about average.

   Some interesting facts emerged from the 'league table'. One schools performance appeared much better than others, but it was discovered that this school was actually sending its students out to a tutorial agency for extra lessons.

10 ORGANIZATION (2)

Writing Tutorial

Confused Writing

Confused writing is not quite the same as rambling writing. Rambling writing does not really have anything to say. Confused writing has many things to say but does not *group the points* and deal with them *one by one in good order*. Confused writing keeps coming back to different aspects of the same points again and again, like a disorganized spider:

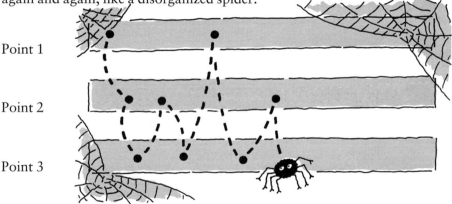

Point 1

Point 2

Point 3

Why does this happen?

When you are speaking, do you ever find that:
- you want to go back to what you were talking about five minutes before?
- you forgot to mention something two minutes ago and now you remember?
- there is something you *must* say now while you remember it?

This is natural. Disorder is natural. But this is one of the differences between writing and speech. *Composition* means ordering and organizing the disorganized thoughts in your head.

It is like any other activity which needs scheduling. If you think about fixing the car while you are having lunch, you do not go straight out and fix the car. You make a mental note about the car and you finish your lunch. *Then* you fix the car. You need to do the same when you write.

Strategies

Soon we'll look at some strategies for dealing with the natural confusion of the mind. But first, we want you to recognize confusion. It is not always easy, but sometimes there are signs which tell you that you are having problems.

TASK 1

Below is a composition about dialects. As you can see, it suffers badly from lack of illustration. It is also not very well organized; in fact, it has at least five warning signs of bad organization. Can you identify them?

> *In my country there are a lot of dialects, I don't know how many, but in every part of the country we can still hear different ways of speaking. Usually we are not able to understand all these dialects, and sometimes they create problems. (Sometimes too people laugh at other people who speak their own dialect in another place.) Anyway, I think that it's important to keep some of these traditional dialects alive. The new generation is not able to speak dialects; in fact, we are losing this form of communication. For this reason it's important to encourage people to continue to speak dialects. In my own town there is a type of dialect and most of the old people use it. We also have some local works of literature written in dialect. By the way, my own town's dialect is so different from other towns that people think it was a separate language in the past. Dialects are an important part of our national history. A lot of people think that speaking a dialect is rough and vulgar and they despise dialect speakers. We should discourage this sort of discrimination and we should encourage the tradition of local dialects, as I said. They are an expression of our culture.*

What do you think the signs are? Think about it, then turn the page round.

Signs

These are some of the warning signs which tell you that you are not getting your thoughts in order:

Brackets ( ) If you find you are putting a long sentence in brackets, you can be fairly sure that it should be somewhere else. Brackets tell you that the sentence may not belong to the point you are making. **Stop and reorganize.**

'As I said before' If you said it before, why are you saying it again? You shouldn't need to use these words in a short composition. **Stop and reorganize.**

'By the way' If it is *by the way*, then it is not *to the point*. You have just thought of it, you feel you must say it. You're probably right, you probably must say it – but not here. **Stop and reorganize.**

'Anyway' This is an expression which suggests that you are coming back to the point. So why did you leave it in the first place? **Stop and reorganize.**

No paragraphs If you haven't used any paragraphs ask yourself why. **Stop and reorganize.**

Sorting and ordering

Even when there are no signs like these, you have to be able to recognize when your thoughts need sorting and ordering.

TASK 2

Practise with someone else's thoughts. Go back to the composition about dialects. The points the writer is making are (very briefly):

1   there are many dialects
2   they create problems of comprehension
3   people laugh at dialect users
4   dialects should be kept alive
5   young people can't speak dialects any more
6   dialects should be encouraged
7   dialect is alive in my town
8   dialects are important in national history
9   people despise dialect speakers
10   we should keep dialects alive
11   they are part of our culture

a   Which points can be grouped together to make *one* idea?
What are the ideas?

b   How would you order the ideas?

c   You should discuss this if possible with other students and/or with your teacher or tutor.

 Check in the Key and compare your ideas.

TASK 3

Here is another example. On the next page is a composition. The writer has a lot to say and it's all very real. But it is confused. It would have much more impact if it was better organized.

Read it through and try to decide how many separate subjects the writer is dealing with, and what they are. Discuss it with others if possible. Make a short list of the subjects below.

_____

_____

_____

_____

_____

Check in the Key before you continue.

> ### MY STUDIES
>
> As regards my examinations at the University, I am very depressed,
> because they are having a negative effect on my life. I am wasting a lot
> of time making several attempts to pass one exam. I find difficulty with
> written exams because they are very complicated. They normally
> consist of three parts: listening, reading and composition, and to pass
> them you need to have a score of six in every test. At present I need to
> pass four examinations to finish my degree: English III, English IV,
> Anglo-American Literature II and Spanish III. In June I would like to do
> English III and Anglo-American II, but I am afraid to take the plunge. I
> am sure I won't pass them.
>
>   I haven't any particular aptitude for learning foreign languages;
> moreover, I am also working (teaching in a private school) and so I
> don't have as much time for studying as I would like. The situation is
> critical. Sometimes I am upset because I know that I have limitations
> and that I must learn a lot. Often I don't understand the dialogue in
> the listening comprehension exam and I start to have a terrible
> confusion in my mind.

TASK 4

Another student wrote about the problems of studying at her university (the
university was just as disorganized as her composition was). She also had a lot to
say. Here is a list of all the points she made, in the order she made them.

Notes for an essay on problems at the university

- ☐ Language teachers should have their contracts in time so that language
  classes can start on time.
- ☐ The University is just a degree factory. It does not really train students for
  jobs or help them to grow personally.
- ☐ Students are isolated from each other.
- ☐ New students don't know how to study and there is no one to help them.
  They need tutorial advice.
- ☐ Students should do an entry test to see if they are good enough to be
  admitted to courses. Attendance can still be optional, as there are students
  who live far away.
- ☐ Language teaching must prepare for examinations. Teachers should have
  similar criteria for every session and year.
- ☐ A modern university should organize international meetings and cultural
  exchanges.
- ☐ The University has few contacts with the world of work.
- ☐ The studies are too theoretical and unrelated to real life – they don't prepare
  students for work.
- ☐ The University should provide work experience opportunities.
- ☐ Jobs require experience and it's very difficult to get experience. Only people
  whose parents have the right sort of contacts can get work experience.

☐ The University should have contact with museums, art galleries, theatres, famous companies, etc.

☐ The University should not have too many students for the places it has. If too many sign on, there is little contact between students and teachers.

☐ A university should have a compact campus, and not be scattered all over the city. This makes it difficult to study properly.

☐ It is also difficult for students to meet other students and discuss things.

☐ The University should help students to make their own choices and decisions so that they can become complete adults and move easily into the working world.

We could classify her points like this:

a   administration
b   personal development
c   admissions policy
d   curriculum
e   social life (contact with other students)
f   geography and layout of the university
g   the university's links with the outside world

The points are clear but she has not grouped them. You do it. Classify each point; give it one of the labels above, e.g. **a**, **b**, etc.

Check in the Key if you are not sure how these points should be grouped.

Preventing confusion

We hope you have seen that, although it is possible to reorganize a confused composition, it takes quite a lot of time – wasted time.

The thinking you have just been doing about these two confused compositions should have come *during the planning*, or during the first draft of the writing, but certainly not after it was written.

Old advice

How do you prevent confused writing? Here's some old advice from the previous units:

1   You have something you want to say and you know what it is. You have an end in mind.
2   You do not start writing straight away.
3   *Before* you start writing you rack your brains, get ideas and illustrations, and prepare your notes.
4   You use your notes to:
    – group points together
    – reject what you don't want
    – decide the best order for the points.
5   Then you start writing your first draft.

But that is not enough.

It is impossible to have all your thoughts before you write. It is nonsense to think that you can plan a composition completely beforehand. You **should** think while you are writing. There **should** be new ideas. There will inevitably be some confusion, some disorganization while you write, as well as before.

New advice

So what do you do about it?

- While you are writing
  - If you think of a new point, make a note of it somewhere else. Do not write it down as the next sentence. You could write your new ideas at the bottom of the page in pencil, then go back to what you're writing.
  - If you think of something you should have said before, don't write it down as the next sentence. Write it at the bottom of the page and put an asterisk (*) or an arrow (↗) to show where it should go.
- After writing, check to see if you have rambled or grouped your points badly. *Edit* – that is, rearrange, cut, move the text around.
- And, finally, write out your final draft and proofread it.

Reading

The fun they had

Education, and what is wrong with it, seem to be the theme of this unit, and also of the short story at the end of the unit. It is by Isaac Asimov, one of the classic writers of science fiction and a master of clear simple narrative.

Asimov is looking at education in the future. Has he got it right? Is this the way the future will or should go?

Think about your own experience. What has changed and is still changing? What *should* change?

ASSIGNMENT 10

EDUCATION

You have a choice of two subjects. You can:

- **write an essay about your study problems like the ones in this unit, or**
- **answer this question: Would you like your children's education to be different from what you received yourself?**

Planning: exam conditions

If you are going to do an exam, we suggest you do this one in exam conditions. Don't use a dictionary. Allow yourself one hour from start to finish. Divide up your time like this:

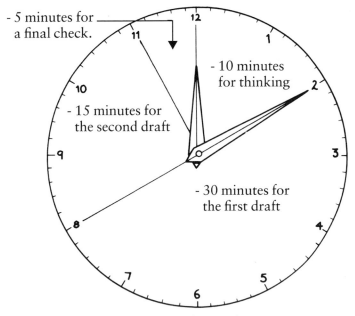

- 5 minutes for a final check.
- 10 minutes for thinking
- 15 minutes for the second draft
- 30 minutes for the first draft

If you wish, ask your reader for a mark out of ten.

ADVICE   *Even in exam conditions you should use your voice to say something that you want to say.*

FEEDBACK

To the reader

Since this is the end of the course, you should read this last composition as if you were an examiner, applying all the criteria we have discussed. If the writer asks you, give a mark out of 10 (6 is satisfactory).

	YES/NO
Does the composition make sense? Is it easy to understand?	
Are the writer's attitudes and feelings clear?	
Is the content interesting?	
Are the points well illustrated?	
Is there a clear structure?	
Is there a strong sense of direction (i.e. no digressions, and an apparently inevitable conclusion)?	
Is the style appropriate, neither too pretentious nor too colloquial?	
Is there a good range of language?	
Do you agree with what the writer says? Please comment.	

Mark out of 10 (if requested) _____

DIARY PROMPT

Who would you like to give some free advice to? People with irritating habits, friends who keep having the same problem, parents or children who don't understand each other, heroes who fall short of your ideals, politicians who have never shared your ideals? Choose one or two and tell them what they ought to do. An 'open letter' might be a good format.

THE FUN THEY HAD

Margie even wrote about it that night in her diary. On the page headed 17 May she wrote 'Today Tommy found a *real* book.'

It was a very old book. Margie's grandfather once said that when he was a little boy his grandfather told him that there was a time when all stories were printed on paper.

They turned the pages, which were yellow and crinkly, and it was awfully funny to read words that stood still instead of moving the way they were supposed to. And then, when they turned back to the page before, it had the same words on it that it had had when they read it the first time.

'Gee,' said Tommy, 'what a waste. When you're through with the book, you just throw it away, I guess.'

'What's it about?' Margie asked.

'School.'

Margie was scornful. 'School? What's there to write about school? I hate school.'

Margie had always hated school, but now she hated it more than ever. The teacher had been giving her test after test in geography and she had been doing worse and worse until her mother had shaken her head sorrowfully and sent for the County Inspector.

He was a round little man with a red face and a whole box of tools with dials and wires. He smiled at Margie and gave her an apple, then took the teacher apart. Margie had hoped he wouldn't know how to put it together again, but he knew how all right and after an hour or so there it was again, large and black and ugly.

The Inspector had smiled after he was finished and patted Margie's head. He said to her mother, 'It's not the little girl's fault, Mrs Jones. I think the geography sector was geared a little too quick. These things happen sometimes. I've slowed it up to an average ten-year level. Actually, the overall pattern of her progress is quite satisfactory.'

Margie said to Tommy: 'Why should anyone write about school?'

Tommy looked at her with very superior eyes. 'Because it's not our kind of school, stupid. This is the old kind of school that they had hundreds and hundreds of years ago.'

Margie was hurt. 'Well, I don't know what kind of school they had all that time ago.' She read the book over his shoulder for a while, then said, 'Anyway, they had a teacher.'

'Sure they had a teacher, but it wasn't a regular teacher. It was a man.'

'A man? How could a man be a teacher?'

'Well, he just told the boys and girls things and gave them homework and asked them questions.'

'A man isn't clever enough.'

'Of course he is. My father knows as much as my teacher.'

'He can't. A man can't know as much as a teacher.'

'He knows almost as much, I bet.'

Margie said: 'I wouldn't want a strange man in my house to teach me.'

Tommy screamed with laughter. 'You don't know much, Margie. The teachers didn't live in the house. They had a special building and all the kids went there.'

'And all the children learned the same thing?'

'Yes, if they were the same age.'

'But my mother says a teacher has to be adjusted to fit the mind of each boy and girl it teaches and that each one has to be taught differently.'

'Just the same, they didn't do it that way then. If you don't like it, you don't have to read the book.'

'I didn't say I didn't like it,' Margie said quickly.

That afternoon Margie went into the schoolroom. It was right next to her bedroom and the teacher was on and waiting for her.

The screen was lit up and it said, 'Today's arithmetic lesson is on the addition of fractions. Please insert yesterday's homework.'

Margie did so with a sigh. She was thinking about the old schools they had when her grandfather's grandfather was a little boy. All the kids from the whole neighbourhood came, laughing and shouting in the schoolyard, sitting together in the schoolroom, going home together at the end of the day. They learned the same things so they could help one another with the homework and talk about it.

And the teachers were *people* . . .

The teacher was flashing on the screen: 'When we add the fractions ½ and ¼ . . .'

Margie was thinking about how the kids must have loved it in the old days. She was thinking about the fun they had.

LANGUAGE TESTS

These two tests are not about composition or writing, but about some of the specific language points practised in the *Language Preparation* part of each unit. The Unit 1 questions in each test relate to the language work for Unit 1; the Unit 2 questions relate to the language work for Unit 2, and so on. The purpose of the tests is to help you find out which points you really need to practise. The answers are all in the Key.

The tests are designed to help you diagnose your problem areas, and think carefully about certain language points. It is *not* important to get a good mark.

You can try all the questions now if you like, or you can do each set of questions (Unit 1, Unit 2, etc.) just before you look at the corresponding language work – which is probably more useful. Or you can do both – which is probably best of all.

TEST A: Grammar/structures

UNIT 1

Put the words in brackets into the sentences. Make any changes necessary, but make as few as possible.

Example   (equipment) We have too *little equipment.*

a   (information) I'd like some _____ .

b   (advice) He gave me several _____ .

c   (work) This is an excellent _____ .

UNIT 2

Underline what you think is the right verb form.

The situation isn't so good. I *haven't done/didn't do* very much of the course yet. I *have had/had* some problems with the second unit: I *haven't understood/didn't understand* some of the points and I *haven't been able to do/couldn't do* one of the exercises. In the end I *have asked/asked* David to help me.
   Anyway, I think *I've understood/I understood* it now and I expect I'll make better progress from now on.

UNIT 3

Fill in the gaps with one or two words.

When Jim and Bill have a conversation, ask them about it afterwards. Jim will tell you what he said, and Bill will tell you what he said, but Jim won't remember what Bill said, and Bill won't remember what Jim said. They don't listen to

_____ , they only listen to _____ .

UNIT 4

In this paragraph there are no definite articles, no *the*s. Put them in wherever you think they are really necessary.

Women's role in society has changed greatly. For example, they now have equal rights in law, and marriage and children are no longer their only option in life: they can also achieve important positions at work. Yet there is a long way to go. If a woman chooses to combine marriage with a career, her problem will probably be time. If she chooses a career instead of marriage, people (even friends) will sometimes consider her strange. Moreover she will need to work very hard to achieve success, since public opinion still sees women as less capable than men, at least at work.

UNIT 5

Which of these words could you use in the spaces below?

SHOULD   WOULD   MIGHT   COULD   WILL   MAY (WELL)

In February Carol was hopeful. She told her friends: 'We [1]_____ go to Rome this year for our holidays. We [2]_____ even go on to Cyprus if we have enough money.'

In April, however, Carol was feeling less optimistic. 'It's going to be rather expensive,' she said. 'We [3]_____ not go to Cyprus at all. We [4]_____ not even be able to go to Rome.'

In June, Carol was in despair. 'We [5]_____ have to give up the idea of Rome. We've got no money. We [6]_____ just about be able to find the fare, but then we'd have nothing left to spend when we got there. So we [7]_____ have to go to Brighton instead.'

UNIT 6

What would you put in the spaces below? (Sometimes more than one answer is correct.)

a   Generally speaking _____ like good food.

      most people   most of the people
      most of people   most the people

b   In general _____ taxis here are yellow.

      the major part of   the most part of
      the majority of   the most of the

c   Generally speaking _____ would like a better job.

      all people   everyone
      all the people   all

d _____ think(s) the death penalty is wrong. Others
support it.

Someone   Some
Some people   Some persons

UNIT 7

The sentences below sound rather like colloquial spoken English. Without
changing the vocabulary, how could you make it more like semi-formal written
English?

I haven't got any exams until June, so I'm feeling very relaxed. My boyfriend's
got a new motorbike and we go out almost every evening. I expect I'll regret it
when June comes, but I'm having a good time now.

UNIT 8

What phrases would you use to show the contrast in these sentences?

a   Most of the children here want orange juice or Coke. The adults,

_____ , usually ask for tea or coffee.

instead   on the other part   on the other hand
however   on the contrary

b   _____ most of the children here want orange juice or Coke,
some of the older ones ask for tea or coffee.

Even if   While   Even though   Whereas
Although   Though   Also if

UNIT 9

Which forms are correct? Mark them with a ✓.

the traffic's problems   the league's policy
the traffic problems   the league policy
the problems of traffic   the policy of the league

Michael's ideas   the work's world
the ideas of Michael   the world of work

UNIT 10

Complete the conversation with appropriate words.

Bob is talking to Mike at length about different sorts of cactus. Suddenly Mike
asks 'What's your girlfriend's name?' Bob can't see the connection. He asks

a   'What does that _____ cactuses?' **or**

b   'What has that _____ cactuses?' **or**

c   'How is that _____ cactuses?'

TEST B: Vocabulary

UNIT 1

Underline the expressions you think are correct.

a   We wasted a lot of time *to go/for going/going* to the wrong office.
b   He spends a lot of money *for/on* clothes and jewellery.
c   I have problems *getting/to get/in getting* to work.

UNIT 2

Look at the picture and complete the sentences.

a   X is _____ Y.
b   That's _____ to walk.

UNIT 3

Which of these expressions would you use in the spaces below?

a   *know   meet   get to know*

I've ¹_____ Angela for five years. We first ²_____
at a party, but then we didn't ³_____ again for some time. One
day we found ourselves sitting side by side in the train and we were able to
⁴_____ each other better.

Which of these expressions would you use to complete the story?

b   *know   find out   discover*

I was surprised to ¹_____ that she already ²_____
a lot about me, while I didn't ³_____ anything about her. So I
started to try to ⁴_____ more about her. The first thing I
⁵_____ was that she was a dancer in a nightclub. By the end of
the journey this was still the only fact I really ⁶_____ for certain
about her. I hadn't, for example, been able to ⁷_____ where she
worked: she wouldn't tell me.

UNIT 4

In the sentence below, can you think of any alternative expressions for *help* and
let?

These funds would *help* us to/*let* us buy advertising time on TV.

UNIT 5

Underline what you think are the correct possible answers.

a Prices have gone up
   in the last few months   in the last months   in recent months
   in the last time   of late   lately
   lastly

b Prices are going up
   nowadays   actually   nowdays
   these days   in these days   at the present
   at present   at the present time

c Prices will go up
   in the near future   in a near future   in the next months
   in the next few months   shortly

UNIT 6

Answer these questions:

a Rachel has twins aged six months, one male, one female. How many sons does she have?

b Marie is 35. Her brother David is 40. Their mother Lucy is 65. Would you say that Marie and David are Lucy's   1 sons,   2 boys,   3 children   4 kids?

c There is a group of people aged 16 to 20 on the street outside. Would you call them   1 boys,   2 children,   3 young people,   4 boys and girls?

UNIT 7

What words would you use in the sentences below to make the points more strongly?

'I would like to [1]_____ that starting a record company is not easy or

cheap. But it is [2]_____ a very interesting and rewarding job.'

UNIT 8

Fill in the spaces with one word or two.

a This woman is talking about her marriage – and only about her marriage.

   I [1]_____ in 1987, so I've [2]_____ for more than

   10 years. I'm married [3]_____ a schoolteacher. It's a terrible

   life. Boring. I'm always thinking of [4]_____ divorced, but it's

   just too much bother.

b   This man is talking about the birth and death of his grandfather.

My grandfather [1]_____ in 1916 and [2]_____ just after

World War Two in 1946. He was just 30 years old when he [3]_____ ,

so he has been [4]_____ for over fifty years.

UNIT 9

In each gap put a word relating to *Politics*.

P_____ go into p_____ not because they want to

put their p_____ into practice, but because they feel at home in

the p_____ world.

In each gap put a word relating to *Economics*.

E_____ study e_____ and know all about the

e_____ forces that rule the world, but they are not always

e_____ with money in ordinary life.

UNIT 10

Below is an opinion. What expressions can you substitute for *I think*? Put a ✓ if
you think the expression is correct.

I think   private schools are not good for children.

By me	In my opinion
To my mind	I'm agree that
As I see it	According to me
I feel that	I would say that
I agree that	I would suggest that

TEACHER'S NOTES

About the course

Nature of the course

The course is written so that it can be used by students working largely on their own, but also by a group in a class or writing workshop. That is, it can stand alone but it can also benefit greatly from group work and teacher input. Apart from this flexibility, the main virtues of the format are:

– the student is given charge of his/her work and knows what s/he is doing and why, and
– the student can do most of the work when s/he feels like it.

Mode of use

You may therefore be using this course in one of several ways:

● **As a tutor**, with the students working mainly on their own. The course was originally piloted in this form. In this case your role is to correct your students' assignments, check feedback work, answer questions about course content and help students evaluate their writing.

● **As the manager of a writing workshop**, with the students working in the same place at the same time, but at their own pace. Here your role is to help and advise with work in progress and to mark finished work. This format is ideal for writing practice: the teacher is freed from up-front teaching, resources such as good dictionaries can be made available to all, students have both their teacher and their peers on call, there is no problem about students missing lessons, and so on. This approach is however expensive in class and teacher time.

● **As a teacher in a conventional classroom** on a 'lockstep' basis, i.e. with a whole class working on the same unit at the same time. The course has also been run in this form. It can be used in two ways:

a **as a taught course**, where the teacher delivers the course content and gives out to the students only the exercises (to be done in class or at home) and the assignments (to be done at home).

b **as a self-taught course** with class backup, where the students work through the units and write the assignments at home and the teacher extends and supplements their work in class with further exercises, remedial treatment, reading, discussion and work on planning writing assignments.

These *Teacher's Notes* are designed for this last case, but will also be useful for tutors or workshop managers.

N.B. *It should be emphasized that the student, the tutor or the teacher can select from the constituents of the course to create a more or less demanding course. This will be clear from the following description of course contents.*

Course contents

Each unit of the course consists of:

● preparatory language work
● a writing tutorial with exercises
● a writing assignment $\Big\}$ **Core**
● advice on planning the assignment
● a feedback questionnaire for the reader
● a reading text
● (from Unit 2 onwards) a diary prompt.

At the back of the book there are also:

● a language entry test
● a key to the test and to the exercises.

Core

The core of the course consists of the writing tutorial and the writing assignment, together with the advice on planning. The other elements are valuable but not essential.

Language work

The preparatory language work does not attempt systematic coverage, but concentrates on single points which often give trouble, many of them closely connected with the work of the unit. The first point in each unit is mainly to do with structure and the second with lexis, and there are also short exercises on prepositions, spelling and punctuation.

The points may be done separately or together, in class or at home, and in any order, but should be covered before the assignment.

N.B. *It should be emphasized that the language work is an optional element in the course, not the main target. There is no instant or automatic bridge between language points* *studied and free written production and students should not be required to produce any specific language in their compositions.*

Reader feedback

Students are advised to have their assignments read by a reader they select themselves (usually another student) before taking them to their tutor/teacher for marking. There are instructions for the reader in each unit. The reader fills in a simple questionnaire to give feedback to the student. The experience of reading and being read is extremely valuable for novice writers, but if the student is working entirely on his/her own, this extra activity may not be possible.

Reading text

To help their language development students should be reading in English while they do the course. The reading passages in this course are mostly non-fiction texts embodying direct experience and/or a personal viewpoint. They have been selected in each case so as to give some particular impetus to the written assignment. They are not however essential to it: if students are already reading a lot in English and do not have much time to spare, this element of the course can be left out.

Diary

Students are given the option in Unit 2 of starting a writer's diary. This will involve the tutor/teacher in some extra marking: you should therefore decide whether you are prepared to take on this extra load.

Language tests

The diagnostic language tests cover the first two language points in each unit. Their purpose is to establish whether students need practice in the specific points dealt with in the units. They also serve as an introduction to the points by raising questions about them: each item of the language tests can therefore act as a lead-in to its corresponding language point.

Course organization

Scheduling

If there is to be a large element of classwork in the course (see page 155), the work on each unit can be spread over two lessons like this (the core elements are in bold text):

Lesson 1
1 remedial work on past assignments
2 reading of latest assignments (if this is to be done in class)
3 preparatory language work
4 **lead-in to next unit**
5 homework: **students work through the unit** and optional language exercises

Lesson 2
1 comments and commendations on previous assignments*
2 **follow-up on the unit**
3 reading text
4 **planning work on the assignment**
5 Homework: **students write the assignment** and do optional language exercises
* *This assumes that teachers will be marking one assignment while students are reading the next unit.*

Time constraints

These elements can be reduced according to time constraints. A skeleton course would consist of only a short lead-in and a short follow-up, with some attention to planning.

Remedial work, assignments, comments, planning work, marking and course records

N.B. *The other elements of the course are dealt with in the notes for each unit, where there are also more detailed notes on planning.*

Remedial work

It is valuable to do some error-correction work from time to time on points which come up frequently. We suggest the very simple procedure below.

● As you mark each set of students' work, pick out five or six sentences which contain very common errors. Simplify or reword the sentences if necessary so that they make sense as they stand and are fairly short. For example:

– *In my opinion there are persons* (people) *who have a gift for writing.*
– *Writing in English doesn't mean translate* (translating) *Italian words into English.*

The errors selected should be real, simple, common and very basic. The ability to recognize and correct errors is much more advanced than correct production, and meeting a whole sentence full of potential errors can send students barking up dozens of wrong trees.

- Write the sentences on the board or OHP, or circulate photocopies. Get students to suggest what's wrong. Let them all consider each suggestion and make up their minds before you tell them if they are right.

- You can also give a selection of the errors dealt with in class as a final test at the end of the course. This is easy to organize and concentrates students' minds wonderfully throughout the course.

Reading of compositions

If peer reading of compositions is to be done in class, before the assignments are handed in, you should remind readers of their current task as outlined in the reader's questionnaire (e.g. to read and react, to identify the strong point), and check that they are doing it conscientiously.

If composition reading is done outside class, ask writers in class to report on some of the reactions they have received: this is a useful check on the kind of comment that is being made. If it will help you to know who reads what, get students to sign the work they read.

Comments and commendations

Students' writing should if possible have a wider audience than just the teacher. Peer reading helps here, but the fact remains that one of a writer's main incentives is the prospect of seeing his/her product in print, in circulation or on display. If possible, arrange for this kind of gratification. Some ideas:

a Post up regularly any assignment or bit of an assignment you particularly like or which receives a high commendation from a reader.

b Ask readers to read out bits they particularly liked.

c Ask students to make a collection of extracts from all the assignments for one unit. This is a nice editing task (regular or one-off). Students work in small groups, reading through each other's assignments, picking out the most usable bits and making any necessary editorial changes. They then copy/paste the selected extracts onto a double-page spread and suggest titles (e.g. *Is writing a bore?/How much do we love money?*). Pictures will also help. The result can be displayed and/or circulated to outsiders.

d Establish a competition for best assignment of the course. Each student submits his/her (self-selected) best assignment; these go into a file which can circulate or be consulted in class. The final judgement is made by the whole class after they have all read everything.

e Students self-select their best assignment for inclusion in the final *Book of the Course*. The book should have everything a book should have – title, foreword, list of contents, etc. Students can do the editing and layout themselves.

N.B. *This project means expensive photocopying if the book is to operate as a proper book and be generally read.*

f The compositions taken collectively have considerable sociological interest. An ambitious but perfectly feasible project for the more competent students is to do a write-up of the class's production on one theme, with quotations, for submission to an English-language magazine.

Planning

It should be emphasized that there is no right way of planning a composition: it is a very individual matter. However, many novice writers don't plan at all: they leap in *in medias res* and often grind to a halt after half a page. The planning advice here aims to get students in the first instance just to *write notes* – in whatever way suits them best – and later to select from them and organize them in preparation for more complex essay-writing.

It is definitely advisable to get students regularly to do some preliminary planning of assignments in class so that you can observe and assist in this process.

Marking

If at all possible, we strongly recommend that you mark assignments (and diary) *together with* the writer. Although it takes slightly longer, it is far more interesting and educational for both of you.

We also recommend that you mark twice – once to correct language errors and the second time for content. These kinds of evaluation do overlap, but are nevertheless quite distinct. We find that double marking sharpens the perceptions of both tutor and writer.

In Unit 4 students are encouraged to make some decisions about the kind of 'feedback work' they want to do with the corrections you make on their work. Their choices may involve you in changing your marking style; you will have to decide if you are willing to do this, and let them know.

Records

Students have a record sheet in their coursebooks on which to record their progress and comment on each unit. You may find it useful to discuss these comments with them.

This record can be a useful indicator to the teacher if combined with other knowledge of the student. For example, you may find it useful to request that students record how long they spend on each assignment. A lot of time spent may indicate a high degree of conscientiousness, or some conceptual difficulty or (if accompanied by many underlinings and glosses) some problems with the language.

If the course leads up to a written exam with a time limit, then the time spent on assignments becomes important, especially in the last few units.

We also suggest you use the *Record Sheet* to write a general comment on each assignment as it is completed: it is invaluable to have an easily accessible summary record of individual students' progress. If you are unable to mark students' work in their company, it is probably best if they make a photocopy of the record sheet and hand it in with each assignment.

Notes for each unit

Notes on Course Introduction and Preliminary Work

The students should have read the Introduction to the course before coming to class.

Follow-up to the Introduction

Explain how you intend to organize the course, e.g. with reading and exercises at home, and follow-up and preparatory work in class.

Reading Discuss whether the reading texts will be:
a read at home and discussed in class
b read in class
c simply read at home, as an option.

Records Discuss the use of the Course Record Sheet.

Marking Indicate how you will be doing the marking, with your students or on your own.

Readers Check that students have found someone to read their work and point out the instructions for the reader in each part. Indicate the importance of being a positive and interested reader.

Reference books Discuss what reference books students will need, giving some advice on the best available dictionaries and grammar books. Students usually need a lot of consciousness-raising about reference books, as well as some practice. There are many useful exercises in existing coursebooks, but the following outline exercises make a good beginning.

Dictionary exercise

Give photocopies of pages covering approximately the same part of the alphabet from:
a a good bilingual dictionary,
b a monolingual reference dictionary (e.g. the *Concise Oxford*) and
c a good learner's dictionary (e.g. The *Oxford Advanced Learner's Dictionary* or *Oxford Wordpower Dictionary*). Then present some of the kinds of question that a writer might have in mind when consulting a dictionary, for example:

What sort of thing would you *curtail*?
a a meal   d someone's power
b a dress   e income
c freedom   f the tail of an animal

Is *curry favour* an expression which is
a approving? **b** neutral? **c** disapproving?

What sort of people *curtsey*?
a men   **b** women   **c** both men and women

Questions like this very quickly demonstrate the strengths and weaknesses of the various sorts of dictionary. The reference dictionary gives derivations and obscure usages, many of which are misleading for the student who only wants the normal usage. The bilingual dictionary gives the referential meaning very quickly but does not usually have the space to show how the word is used. The learner's dictionary gives the commonest meanings and exemplifies them; it also gives other lexical and grammatical information essential to a second-language writer.

Grammar books

A rough-and-ready test of how easy a reference grammar is to use is to select a few small problems which students are aware of and try to locate them in a number of grammar books, including the students' own. This can be enjoyable if students suggest the problems and other students race to find them – the race being between one grammar book and another rather than between the students. Emphasize that the problem must be very small and specific and give a few examples:

– the plural of *person*
– structures with *wish*
– the uses of *used to*.

Lead-in to Preliminary Work

Use the first page of Preliminary Work as a basis for class discussion: individuals or small groups (or both) work to formulate their arguments and then report to the whole class. Students should then do the rest of the Preliminary Work, and the Preliminary Writing at home. Remind them to get their work read before handing it in.

Follow-up to Preliminary Work

At the following lesson ask about the priorities students selected and briefly discuss class or individual hang-ups and ambitions to do with writing.

Marking

The Preliminary Writing should give you some idea of how your students feel about writing. It will be a product unaffected by instruction, so you will be able to see just how good your students are already and what they need to learn in terms of language, layout and presentation, organization and interest. You may want to report back to them once you have read all their work.

UNIT 1

Lead-in

Find a composition which looks bad (obviously it should not be traceable to any known student) or write your own on a scrap of dirty paper torn from a notebook. Wave it around and ask what is wrong with it. Emphasize that you are concerned at the moment only with *visual* impact – presentation and layout.

Get students to identify the inadequacies of your MS and the English terms for them, e.g. bad handwriting, crossing out, wrong paper (also *coloured* paper), no margin. Then ask for a description of what a finished piece of work looks like. Write up the rules they suggest. Do not comment.

Indicate that the conventions of layout in English may be slightly different from theirs: they will discover this in their homework reading. If there are any other aspects of presentation that you require of the students, feel free to change the course's 'document presentation requirements' at this point.

Follow-up

It may be weeks before all your students conform to all the document presentation requirements. They tend to overreact in some directions and underreact in others. But they will get the habit in the end.

● Check that students remember the useful expressions on page 19 (*cross out, asterisk*, etc.)

● Check the rewrite exercise on page 21 in class. Lazy students who copy the words from page 20 will not only have passed up the revision opportunity but will also have the wrong wording.

Reading text: Money

Warm-up

Start with all the things you can do with money, e.g. *get it, earn it, give it away, spend it, exchange it for other currencies, save it, hoard it, count it, bury it, waste it, lend it, borrow it, beg it, steal it, embezzle it, forge it, invest it, pay taxes on it.*

Read and discuss

It is useful to introduce the questionnaire by explaining the classifications it is based on (materialist/unworldly, etc. – see the Key). Then allow them to work through it as suggested in their notes. Small group work is particularly desirable because an important purpose of the exercise is to see how people differ in their attitudes and behaviour.

Bridge to assignment

Do money attitudes run in families? Do their own attitudes come from imitating their families or reacting against them? How do they feel about their siblings' ways with money? Demand examples of specific behaviour.

Planning work

Students should do some assignment planning in class so that you can discuss ideas with them and see what they do: it can be an eye-opener. The suggestion here is that students make some notes. We are trying to prevent two tendencies:

a to leap into writing the beginning of the composition without considering direction
b to think that notes consist of full sentences.

We suggest random jottings, on the principle that free thoughts usually start in chaos. Later in the course students are asked to select and organize, but for the moment we only want them to *make normal scrappy notes*. Get them to see that they can save time by not producing full sentences, and try to get them to loosen up and use the white space on the page freely. Write your own notes on the board so that they can see what notes look like.

Marking

This assignment is not one with a self-evident organization, so it should reveal to you which students have some feeling for form and which ones produce strings of disconnected sentences. Look for thoughts carried over several

sentences, expressions which mark changes of subject, generalizations followed by illustrations and conclusions which sound conclusive.

UNIT 2

Lead-in

Find a sample of *hot air* (not from an identifiable student, of course) or write one yourself or use the following. Circulate it or display it.

> It is tragic these days to see and hear about so much crime on the streets. How can young people do these things? I think they must be crazy. If you look into their faces you would never believe that they are really violent criminals who have beaten old men and women or taken away all the money from poor people.
>
> Is all this crime the fault of our society? What can we do to stop this evil? Can we only look on helplessly? I am only a student and I don't know the answer to these heavy questions. Perhaps education will help young people to see that crime is not the way to happiness.

Indicate that the English is correct, and invite criticisms of the *content*. If this is a long time coming, ask students to ask questions about any points that are not completely clear, or of which they are not completely convinced. Some questions might be:

- *What crime in particular?*
- *Why pick on young people?*
- *Why doesn't the writer try to find out why they do it?*
- *Has the writer really looked into their faces? How does s/he know what they look like?*
- *Why does the writer choose to mention old and poor people? Are they the normal victims of crime? Is this just to raise cheap emotion?*
- *Why ask so many questions and not answer any of them?*
- *Will education really help? Why isn't it helping now?*
- *Who says crime is not the way to happiness?*

Ask the group to try to diagnose the *main problem* of the writer – which is, essentially, that s/he has nothing to say, is marking time, filling space, churning out platitudes, generating hot air. Pick up the message that *writing should have something to say.*

Writer's diary

This unit introduces the idea of keeping a writer's diary, which you may want to encourage or discourage. We have found that it is very motivating and it does give practice and extend vocabulary; it also gives the teacher many insights into students' lives. It has not so far brought to light any major literary talent, but you may be lucky.

Follow-up

- Check that they diagnosed the *hot air* exercise correctly.
- Discuss the idea of the diary. Find out who wants to keep one and indicate whether you are willing to mark it.
- **Hoax**   If you have time, play the game *Hoax*. The idea is simple: three people tell stories about interesting things which happened to them: two of the stories are totally true and one is false. After each story, the audience can question the story-tellers, but must reserve judgement till the end, when they have to decide which story is the hoax.

  Ask three volunteers to prepare stories for the following lesson. They must agree among themselves who is to be the hoaxer and in what order they will tell their stories.

  If the game goes well it will furnish material for discussion on what makes a story convincing – if only its tedium!

Reading Text: First Day Off

Warm-up

- The Big City: for you, where is it? Have you had the experience of coming to the big city from a smaller place? Did you have any illusions?
- How did you cope – were you humble and ignorant or did you pretend to know your way around? Did you ask questions or find out beforehand?
- Have you ever been lost in a city? How did it happen?

Read and discuss

- This text lends itself to serial reading. From the end of the second paragraph doom is clearly on its way: invite predictions. After paragraph 4 it's possible to anticipate most of the conversation with the bus conductor.

After paragraph 6 encourage a little speculation about the outcome, then read to the end.

- Go back and trace the changes of mood and the reasons for them. Find the words which reveal mood – 'I thought, oh well …' 'very seedy …' 'dirty little shops …' 'you bloody well won't see it …' 'crestfallen'.
- Locate the central moment (when the bus conductor tells her she has taken the wrong bus) and notice how it is expanded and slowed down by being put into dialogue.
- Get the students to rough out a 'mood graph', something like this:

Then elaborate the diagram, labelling the events and defining the feelings, e.g.

beginning of the journey
excited anticipation
the buildings and seedy neighbourhood
slight disappointment etc.

Planning

Discuss preliminary ideas and check that students are producing some kind of notes. Discuss the stories and demand details. Encourage them to try out their stories on each other. They should also be trying to set a focus to the writing, a high point or low point. If they are clever they can give it some 'drag' as in the Powell story.

Marking

Above all, you are looking for something which sounds real and manages to get across some of the feelings experienced.

UNIT 3

Lead-in

Do the first exercise in class because it benefits from an exchange of opinions. Give the students at least fifteen minutes to make up their minds, individually or in small groups. Discuss their ranking and their criteria, then move on to the examiners' comments on page 45 and see whether you agree.

N.B.   *There is no reason why you yourself should agree with the examiners.*

Ask the students to suggest:

a   what criteria the examiners may be applying and

b   which criteria the examiners have apparently prioritized.

Leave the rest of the unit to be done at home.

Follow-up

- Review the criteria discussed and indicate where your personal priorities lie: this will be important to students if you are their main assessor.
- If students are heading for an examination, they will need information about exam contents and criteria; this is a good time to discuss where to find it.
- Check that students have done the self-evaluation and make arrangements for giving your own parallel evaluation of their work to date. Individual appointments are best.

Reading text: Babe Secoli

Warm up

Ask students to say what manual jobs they have done and what they were like. Then speculate on the potential agony, boredom or interest of being a checker in a supermarket.

Read and discuss

- After reading, recapitulate Babe's *skills* (knowledge of prices, speed, nose for shoplifters, tact); *annoyances* (fatigue, varicose veins, rude customers); and *pleasures* (in her abilities and in the customers' quirks). Discuss anything unexpected.
- Reactions to Babe: admirable/pathetic/interesting/just ordinary? Sum up the response in one sentence.
- Which of her words give the best impression of what she is like? Underline them and discuss.

Bridge to assignment

The last two points above suggest two ways of ending a composition – with a summary evaluation, or with a characteristic quotation. These can lead in to the written assignment.

Planning work – notes

As students write their notes, ask individuals for *details* of the person they have chosen: what acts/sayings/looks/gestures do they remember? Collect *good details* on the board (e.g. She is a fantastic cook, especially for sweets/He seems shy because he is very short-sighted).

This time students should try to select an ending before they start writing: this stops them using up all their good material in the first five minutes. Do not insist on it, however – often the idea for a good ending comes as one writes.

Marking

Again we are looking for the strength of real-life observation – as well as for a good ending. You should also be evaluating the writer's general strengths and weaknesses in terms of the criteria discussed in the unit.

UNIT 4

Lead-in

Use any (unattributable) short composition with a number of basic errors, or composition B in the previous unit. Ask students to put themselves in the position of a teacher/tutor. What would they do with it? Correct? Comment? Grade? They should then quickly mark the work (individually or in groups), neglecting any points they are not sure of, and write a comment at the end.

Follow up by discussing (in this order):
- whether they used pencil or pen, and what colour, and why
- what comments they wrote
- what they corrected and how.

Concentrate on correctness, traditionally the major concern of marking. Pick a few of the more basic errors for example (from Composition B):

a old man . . . *a old* song
a *point black* on the left eye
it *do* a lot of things
the south *caost*
he *tracks* the *attencion*
the show *beging*
All people are *attonit for* the little dog
others children

Ask the students now to change viewpoint and put themselves in the position of students receiving the marked work. What would they do about these errors? Applaud mentalistic approaches ('I would try to understand the corrections') but also require them to say what they would *physically do*. Do not comment, but ask them to work through the rest of the unit for homework.

Follow-up

In the unit students are expected to arrive at a decision about the kind of feedback they would like. In the meantime you should decide how far you are prepared to accommodate their requests. Two of the suggestions for feedback work (Induction I and II) would involve you not only in a different sort of marking (and in establishing a code) but also in checking students' diagnoses at a later stage (I find they are only about 40% correct). You may want to negotiate these points with your students.

The various 'feedback work' prescriptions may seem obvious and easy to follow, but you will need to check students' remedial work at least twice to make sure they are doing something genuinely productive. Left to themselves, some do nothing, some copy out individual words meaninglessly and some in an excess of zeal copy out the whole composition.

To forestall the worst excesses do some preparatory work now. Go back to the errors you identified in Composition B and work on some of the ways of using feedback.

a **Re-writing I**   Correct the mistakes and ask students to write out the correct forms. Emphasize the idea of writing out the appropriate *phrase* – just enough to remind you of the context of the error. For example:

an old man NOT   ~~a old~~

b **Collecting points**   Select a few points for students to write messages about. Again, emphasize economy and clarity, e.g. spelling mistakes can just be listed under 'Spelling' and some errors can be brought together. An error message for the writer of composition B might read:

Adjectives come before the noun and they don't agree with it –
1   2   3
a black point
other children

c **Induction**   Those who want to try the induction approaches are often bright and adventurous; they need to realize however

that they *must* get their guesses checked. Get this point home with composition A in Unit 3. Number the lines and give a coding for some of the more obvious errors, e.g.

l.9 WO (= word order; indirect question)
*l.10 V (= vocabulary, **made** should be **done**)*
*l.11 V (**works** should be **jobs**, or **work**)*
*l.12 V (**possibilities** should be **opportunities**
        or **chances**)*
l.13 WO (indirect question)

Let them see if they can diagnose and correct them all.

Reading text: A streetcar named Desire

Warm-up

To focus attention on representative behaviour ask students what behaviour they would expect from house guests and hosts – for example in terms of dealing with luggage, giving presents, contributing to household expenses, being polite, using the telephone, taking people out, cooking, etc. Then read to see how this host and guest behave.

Read and discuss

We suggest each student takes one part and prepares it silently, considering how the words should be spoken. The extract should then be read aloud at least twice, and different interpretations discussed. N.B. the word 're-bop' is not in the dictionary: we leave it open to creative interpretation.

Discuss

a Do Blanche or Stanley do any of these things?
  flirt flatter overdramatize conciliate
  bully boast insult apologize
  Where exactly?

b Does either of them show:
  contempt brutality vanity sentiment
  jealousy cynicism naiveté rudeness irony
  tact hostility self-control
  Where exactly?

c Blanche feels she's handled it well. Has she?

d How do you react to these two characters and their behaviour? Is this the sort of behaviour that really annoys you? If not, what does?

Planning work

For this composition, students are recommended to chart their notes on a table –

partly for variety, and partly to make visible the importance of illustrative support. The three columns oblige students to think of specific people and behaviour in relation to their general ideas – and *vice versa*.

The device is meant to be a prop, not a prison, so dispel anxieties about what students 'have' to do. There are no rules – only the three columns. Prime the pump by 'thinking aloud' your own three columns on the board. While students are gathering ideas, pick out a few more good examples and get their creators to write them up.

Marking

You are looking for very simple organization (not necessarily marked with paragraphs) and also (we hope) some explicit transition from the vices to the virtues, or *vice versa*. Some vivacious supporting illustration would also be nice.

UNIT 5

A note on paragraphing

If students have not been used to paragraphing, do not expect too much at first. The habit will come gradually, starting with the physical layout.

There are a lot of valuable exercises in modern coursebooks on recognizing main points in well-organized texts; some can be used to supplement this unit. They do not, however, always help students to recognize the points that they themselves are making, often sentence by sentence. This is the purpose of the note-taking exercise recommended in the follow-up.

It should also be recognized that English paragraphs are not as standardized as is sometimes suggested; they have different forms and functions in different kinds of discourse (e.g. stories, news items, letters). The one-idea paragraph with a topic sentence is perhaps most often found in academic writing and reports.

Lead-in

Refer to any readily available text (textbook, newspaper, this course). Ask students to look at the page layout and describe it, then concentrate on the paragraphs.

– How many paragraphs are there?
– How are they identified?
– How many sentences are there on average in one paragraph?
– How many single-sentence paragraphs?
– What are the paragraphs for? Get some ideas.
– Do they matter?

Follow-up

- Check tasks – Task 3 in particular – and discuss the paragraphing in Tasks 4 and 5. It should become clear that paragraphing is a question of judgement more than rules, but that some solutions are more justifiable than others.
- Draw students' attention to the reader's task for this unit – to say if the paragraphs reflect the parts of the composition. To help with this, practise making notes on the paragraphs identified in Tasks 4 and 5, for example:

Task 4
Girls' dreams
Nice life: lots of help   busy/glamorous social lif
Reality: no private life   no career

Task 5
Terrorists allowed to leave jail: reasons in favour
Argument against: criminals must pay
Summary conclusion (nasty prisons prevent crime

Reading text: Beware the Eurogook

Warm-up

- What is unreadable: textbooks, some newspapers, official forms? Make a list and discuss which are the worst – who would you give the prize to?
- What makes them unreadable: boring content, genuine complexity, style/language?
- Can anything be done about it – seriously? The text is about someone who did something.

Read

Interview If you have time for an extra activity, suggest that to get into the right fighting spirit, and to review comprehension, students should put themselves into Chrissie Maher's shoes and prepare to be interviewed about the PEC. As with all media interviews they should know in advance the questions that will be asked (photocopy or display):

- Now, Mrs Maher, would you tell us very briefly what the PEC is about? What exactly is its purpose?
- How did you personally first come into contact with the problem?
- So when did the Campaign begin?
- And how did you launch the Campaign? What was your very first move?
- Did it have the kind of immediate effect you wanted?
- Now, I believe that the government has actually employed your organization to educate its civil servants and the members of Parliament about plain English. What exactly have they asked you to do?
- So the Campaign is in fact funded by the Government?
- After all your efforts, do you think the Civil Service has really made any tangible progress with its forms? Is it possible to quantify the results?
- Finally, what about the future? What is the next battle, and where?

Students can rehearse and perform the interview, or respond in turn to the teacher as interviewer, or write the answers.

Discuss

What were the tactics and strategies of the campaign and the reasons for their success?

Main strategy: High publicity/media impact (the initial provocative shredding, the exhibitions, the publication *Gobbledygook*). Choice of government as a target.

Other probable tactics not mentioned: the follow-up the Campaign may have mounted – e.g. circular letters to government ministries, petitions, objections to particular forms, possibly even civil disobedience (always with media coverage).

Reasons for success: sense of shame generated in culprits; obvious popular appeal; receptive attitude of government; Chrissie Maher's personal experience of people's problems, including her own; self-financing activities; genuine value to all, including bureaucrats.

Planning work

Here we are militating against one kind of hot air, the unconstructive complaint. Students often write a long complaint about some vast and acceptably awful problem (traffic,

environmental pollution, war) and neglect the action programme. We therefore emphasize *relevance*, that is, covering the subject as given, including the second half, and we ask students to limit themselves to small and manageable civic targets (e.g. the glue on postage stamps, the quality of street lighting).

Discuss the feasibility of students' campaign ideas in class; this will also help the less imaginative students. Encourage all ideas for concrete action (use of local TV stations and newspapers, demos, lobbying MPs, working through political parties and other organizations, letter-writing campaigns, etc.). If several people have the same idea, let them work it out together.

Marking

As suggested to the student reader, the main criteria are relevance, imagination and a realistic feeling for cause and effect (you may find that cause and effect vocabulary makes a useful subject for remedial work).

UNIT 6

Lead-in

The 'brainracking' of this unit is the individualized version of group brainstorming, a technique you should now introduce. Ask what students do when they can't get ideas. Suggest that the problem is not absence of ideas but inaccessibility, and that what's needed is some shaking up of the brain.

Demonstrate brainstorming in three stages:

a **Generating ideas** Take one of the unit's assignment subjects (or any other subject). Pin up or draw an appropriate picture in the middle of the board, ask for *all* ideas that come to mind, and write them up randomly around the picture. Emphasize that all ideas are acceptable.

b **Organizing** When the flood becomes a trickle, stop and spend another ten minutes grouping ideas into a mind-map.
See page 166 for an example.

c **Selection** Emphasize that this is *not* an essay plan. A map is a map, an essay is a personal journey to a destination. Get students to say which area of the map is of particular interest to them and could expand into their *own* composition. Contribute your own idea (mine, for example, is a story of unsuccessful attempts to get rid of mice, and the humanitarian agonies involved).

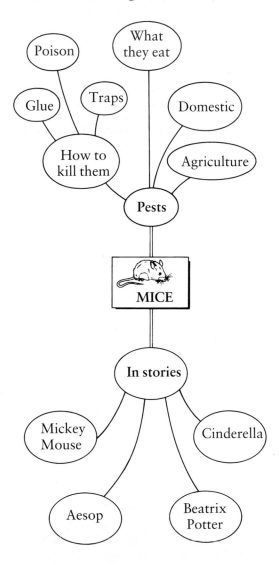

Follow-up

● Follow up on Task 1 by asking which of the two composition planners students resemble. Flatter both: divergent thinkers are (or may be) fertile in ideas while convergent thinkers have (or may have) powerful control.
● In Task 2, check that students have **a** genuinely let themselves loose on the subject of **mice** or **mountains**, **b** identified their *own* main idea (with supporting ideas) and **c** decided on their own ending.

Reading text: The Green Hat

Students often fail to make connections between themselves and what they read: they see given texts as a gospel to be memorized or repeated and not as something intended to affect their own behaviour, as this one is. Whether De Bono is right or wrong doesn't really matter as long as he can persuade his readers to experiment and see what happens.

Warm-up

What different kinds of thinking might there be, i.e. what do the other five 'hats' represent? Ask what message they expect and how they expect to be personally affected by it.

Read

This should be silent individual reading focused on finding the message.

Discuss

What do they think of the examples of green-hat thinking (e.g. pensions for ex-prisoners)? If they find them silly, this is as it should be – licence is the name of the game in green-hat thinking. Nothing is rejected, nothing is criticised.

Bridge to assignment

What is the message? That they should always 'set aside time for deliberate creative thinking'.

Planning work

Suggest small groups based on the choice of assignment subject. Supply two large pieces of paper per group, one for idea generation and one for organizing the ideas. Emphasize that an essay can't be written by a committee: the social activity must finally lead to an individual choice and each person should leave the group with his/her *own* idea on paper.

Marking

What you are hoping for is simply more, and more interesting, ideas. My experience is that when idea-generation activities are successful, some students have trouble selecting and organizing their material, and there is a temporary lapse in organization. I would not hammer the virtues of coherence until they have adjusted to the technique.

Feedback check

As a follow-up, it is advisable to check that students are not only doing 'feedback work' but also doing it sensibly and economically.

UNIT 7

Lead-in

There are two issues here. Naive writers with little experience of writing in their own language will be moving from speech forms to writing. More sophisticated writers will be learning to recognize the permissible range of style in English compared to their L1. You may need to raise consciousness in both areas.

Speech vs writing Discuss superficial differences (visible/audible; spelling and punctuation; speed; distance from audience; specific vs general audience). Then distribute the two short texts below. Both represent 'real speech', though with different transcription conventions. Get different groups to edit them into an acceptable 'written' form and, as they do so, ask them to list all the *kinds* of change they have to make.

a *it's erm – an intersection of kind of two – a kind of crossroads – of a minor road going across a major road – and I was standing there – and there was this erm – kind of ordinary car – on the minor road – just looking to come out – onto the big road – and coming down towards him on the big road was a van – followed by a lorry – now – just as he started to come out onto the main road – the van – no the lorry star-started to overtake the van – not having seen the fact that another car was coming out*

b *we had a fantastic time – there were all kinds of relations there I dunno where they all come from I didn't know 'alf of them – and ah – the kids sat on the floor – and ol' Uncle Bert he ah o' course he was the life and soul of the party Uncle Bert 'ad a black bottle – an' ah – e'd tell a few stories an' e'd take a sip out of the black bottle 'n the more sips he took outa that bottle – the worse the stories got –*

Possible answers:

a I was standing at an intersection of a minor road with a major road. An ordinary car was just about to come out onto the big road.

Coming towards him on the big road was a van, followed by a lorry. Just as (the car) started to come out onto the main road, the lorry started to overtake the van, not having seen that another car was coming out.

b We had a fantastic time. There were all kinds of relations there: I don't know where they all came from – I didn't know half of them. The children sat on the floor, and old Uncle Bert was of course the life and soul of the party. Uncle Bert had a black bottle, and he'd tell a few stories and he'd take a sip out of the black bottle. And the more sips he took out of that bottle, the worse the stories got.

Discuss the changes made. Obvious changes are:
– omitting false starts, hesitations, rephrasings, pauses
– using conventional spelling and punctuation.

More debatable changes are:
– omitting approximations (e.g. *kind of*)
– standardizing the grammar (e.g. *where they all come from*)
– removing colloquialisms (e.g. *kids*)
– conflating strings of simple sentences.

Look at the two final versions together. Which one is still closer to speech? In fact, *Uncle Bert* remains irresistibly spoken English. Some of the reasons are:
– familiarity (*that bottle, old Uncle Bert*)
– exaggeration (*fantastic/I didn't know half of them*)
– vagueness (*all kinds of/a few*)
– repeated constructions (*he'd . . . he'd*).

N.B. *Do not let students start thinking that written language is in some way 'better' than speech. Both are appropriate in their own contexts. It is disastrous if students start to speak like books, for example when giving talks in class. Moreover, it is likely that their own spoken English is in desperate need of the very features that characterize* **Uncle Bert**.

L2 vs L1 styles If you have time for this, ask students to find for the following lesson two or three short L1 prose texts which illustrate the range of styles available to L1 writers (newspapers, official documents, art criticism and tourist literature may be good sources) or which they consider stylistically typical. They should translate them into English.
Number and circulate the texts the students bring, then discuss how well their styles translate into English.

Follow-up

- Check that students have absorbed the terminology of the unit – the four kinds of artificial emphasis, the meaning of *sloppy wording* and the five points – tautology, internal contradiction, over-generalization, loose wording and mixed metaphor.
- For Task 4, check that students were able to recognize the problems (some can't), then go through their improved versions, where these differ from the Key.

Reading texts: Jargon and slang

A lot can be done with this assortment. The priorities are, first, for students to see the *point* of each item, and then to decide, as independently as possible, how they personally feel about the language it deals with.

Read

Let students browse, ask questions and comment.

Discuss

Identify the kind of language targeted in each item – bureaucratic nomenclature, slang and swearing. Pick out examples in each case. Get students to explain the point of *How Many It Takes* (the satirical inflation of a simple domestic act).

Focus

Ask students to select *one* of these two texts for a closer focus.

- *How Many It Takes* can enjoyably be 'translated' into the actual scenario it represents, e.g.
  - (Sally) notices the light bulb is dim (compared to other lights)/She decides to change it for a 100-watt bulb/She asks if everyone agrees/She gets some money (etc.)
  - Draw up a list of formal and informal equivalents (e.g. *buy* – *acquire, purchase*)
  - Also list the words which give the work titles their bogus sonority – *expert, analyst, personnel, 'official' lightbulb changer* – and discuss equivalent titles in their own language. Why do people use these words?
- **Australian slang** Ask students to explain the less obvious items and get their reactions to the sardonic tone of *face fungus* and *rug rat*, the idea of rhyming slang, and the ubiquitous Australian habit of shortening

words. Get them to invent sentences (e.g. *That drongo is still watching the idiot box.*) Do they enjoy slang? What do they think characterizes Australian slang? Why do people use slang? Do they use a lot of slang in their own language?

Bridge to assignment

Finally, students should describe features of accent, dialect and pronunciation in their own language or in English and say how they feel about them and why.

Planning work

Brainstorming and brainracking need practice. We suggest you go through the same group procedure as in the last unit, again with a generative phase, an organizing phase, and a selection and development phase, either in class or in groups. Resist the temptation to organize students' ideas as they offer them: they need the mental exercise.

Insist on examples. Adopt a different colour chalk or boardpen to distinguish examples from ideas. Given the subject of the composition, it is particularly appropriate to beg for quotations; you may also like to anticipate the next unit by demonstrating how quotations should be punctuated.

Marking

The focus of the unit is of course an appropriate semi-formal style, but by now you can begin to hope for the magic combination of fresh ideas, simple visible organization and interesting illustrative support.

UNIT 8

Lead-in

The idea of illustration is most vividly demonstrated with an item from a TV news broadcast, in which the text is "illustrated" variously by stills, clips and quotations from talking heads. (The CBS or CNN News, which are broadcast in many countries, usually have good clear-cut examples.) A good exercise is to listen to or read the text, without vision, and think how it could be illustrated, then view the full version, and discuss the number and types of illustration.

Alternatively, take a page of a newspaper which has a good number of memorable pictures – if possible:

a a dramatic photograph of a news event
b a dramatic story with big headlines but no photograph and
c an advertisement with a striking picture.

Your questions will depend on what you have. Here are some possibilities:

a (After displaying the page briefly and putting it away) What was on the page?
b (Displaying the page again) Which article would you read first? Why?
c What can you tell about the advertisement from the picture?
d How much of the page is devoted to pictures?
e What would it be like with no pictures?
f What is the purpose of each picture?

The aim is to bring out the attraction, high impact, informative power and memorability of pictures (in the news adage, *one picture is worth a thousand words*, or, as Alice in Wonderland put it, *What is the use of a book without pictures or conversations?*).

Make the connection with writing. A writer also needs the power of pictures to bring the text to life. Pictures in writing are *illustrations* – comparisons, metaphors, examples, quotations.

Follow-up

To recap the main points of the unit, read out the Dracula quotations and ask what is the point of each one. Some students have genuine difficulty distinguishing an example from the point it illustrates. Check whether they had any problems with Task 2.

Discuss the illustrations and particulars they have suggested for Tasks 4, 5 and 6.

Reading text: *The Hurled Ashtray*

Warm-up

Prepare the vocabulary listed in the students' text. 'Translate' *Wouldja mind sayin' that agin?*; get students to try it out in different tones (polite, threatening, laid-back) and suggest appropriate situations.

Focus on traditional Hollywood male stereotypes in old movies (e.g. Westerns). How did the all-male hero behave towards women? (Protective, possessive, decisive, strong, brave.)

How did the women respond? (Timid, adoring, flattered, sometimes cheeky or resistant, but eventually submissive.)

Read, visualize and discuss

Read the first paragraph (the Cooper story) and get reactions. Can students visualize the scene (it is straight out of a Western)? What makes it so classic? (The understatement, the deliberation, the confidence, the casual movement.)

Read paragraphs 2 and 3 (the Korda story). If your students enjoy a bit of action, do a slow walk-through of the scene, with full cast, token props (tray, card, ashtray), all actions (sniggering, tearing up card, etc.) and suitable ad-libbed script.

Pause to discuss:
– the differences between Cooper's and Korda's behaviour
– what they think of Mr Korda's behaviour
– what they think of Mrs Korda's behaviour
– what they would have done themselves.

Finally, read to the end and discuss the reactions of Nora Ephron and her friends.

Bridge to assignment

Is this the fight that women should be fighting? If not, what? Would you personally like men/women to behave differently? If so, *how*?

Planning work

Now that students have got the idea of brainstorming, they can decide whether they get their ideas best in groups, or in pairs, or alone. In any case they must ultimately develop their own composition outlines individually.

With the move to less personal subjects, the danger of trite generalizations is magnified. We have to insist that **what happens to the individual** is a bridge to general interest. Pull out good examples from students' planning notes, and contribute your own observations. For example, an Italian student once told me how her mother still peels fruit for her brother (aged 32) after meals, a striking example of the attention Italian men expect at home.

Marking

Look especially for good illustration supporting a few clear ideas, and the ability to make a personal voice heard through a semi-formal style.

UNIT 9

Lead-in

Play *Sequitur*, a variant of Consequences.
Each person in a small group has a blank sheet
with one sentence at the top – for example:

- *Always lock your door when you go out of
  the house.*
- *Interior decoration looks so easy.*
- *The death penalty is still in force in parts of
  the US.*
- *Perhaps love of animals is a sign of immaturity.*
- *Some people have extraordinary ideas about
  diet.*

No one knows what the others' sentences are.
The idea is to produce a paragraph in which
each sentence is inspired only by the one before
it. Each person studies his/her sentence, writes
the next sentence, then folds over the paper so
that only the last sentence is visible and passes
it on. This is repeated until each paper has gone
full circle, then the papers are unfolded and the
results are read out. The prize goes to the
paragraph which has wandered furthest from
the original subject.

Follow-up

Check on alternative endings to the composition
in Task 2. They should generally be on the theme
of *Is modelling worth it?* or *A short life but a
happy one* or *The image is better than the reality.*

Take this occasion to circulate or display
some good beginnings and endings from
students' output so far and say why you like
them. Ask if students have any other
techniques for ending.

Reading text: Testimony

Students should be moving towards essays with
an argumentative structure, in which
conclusions follow from and are supported by
evidence and illustration. The tight purposeful
construction of courtroom questioning is a
model in this respect.

Warm-up

- Reminisce a little on courtroom film dramas.
- The purpose of courtroom questioning (not
  cross-questioning): to get witnesses to tell
  their stories in their own words (counsel
  must not lead the witness) and at the same
  time to order and control the questioning so
  that a significant conclusion can be drawn.

Read

Intelligent students will link Alabama, civil
rights and the vote and realize that this must be
a case of racial discrimination operating
through bureaucracy. Students cover the last
two questions and answers. Discuss the precise
purpose of the questioning, and what the final
questions and answers might be before looking
at them.

Discuss

Feelings   Discuss the feelings of the witness at
the time and now. Rage? Scepticism? Despair?
Determination? Indignation? Why does the
courtroom event by contrast sound so cool?
Was it as cool as it sounds?

Control   Divide the first part of the text as
shown below and discuss the exact purpose of
each section (purposes are suggested).

Lines

1–3	Establish citizenship and age qualifications.
4–9	Establish residency qualifications.
10–16	Establish general respectability – professional and married status.
17–22	Deal with military service – presumably to demonstrate that Mr Hunter served his country.
23–38	Establish literacy qualifications (well in excess of any minimum standards) as well as general respectability – membership of scholastic societies counts as a 'character reference'.
39–40	Church membership is a further character reference.
41–42	Establish that Mr Hunter cannot be disqualified on grounds of insanity.
43–44	Establish that Mr Hunter cannot be disqualified on grounds of criminal convictions.
45 *ff.*	Establish that correct procedure has been followed in applying to register for the vote.

Planning work

We would suggest that students work on their
own to decide what they want to say and how
to shape their writing. But it will help if you
can demonstrate the range of events covered by
the word 'injustice'. Going back to the
childhood concept of what's 'not fair' should
produce a number of examples. Most comedy
films (try *Fawlty Towers*) have scenes which
illustrate multiple personal injustices, while the
newspapers are full of professional indignation

about real horror stories. If possible, give an anecdotal example of your own.

Marking

Writers have had quite a lot of help with the planning of this composition. It should:
a be pinned down to one or more real cases
b have a solid overall structure and
c stick firmly to the subject.

UNIT 10

A note on organization

The need for the ability to sort and order ideas is not very apparent as long as students are writing short compositions on simple subjects and getting some guidance with the structure, but becomes very evident with longer more discursive essays written independently. Here you may run into a problem of credibility.

Some students are almost completely unaware of the concept of organizing, ranking and sequencing ideas. Others are aware that organization is something desired by their teacher but are not at heart convinced of its value; some also find the organizing process boring and alien, even painful.

We should be sympathetic to these feelings. The need for organizing ideas can only be felt through a great deal of experience of handling them. Normally the ability and the need for it grow side by side and in some cases English classes are the only place where students are being required to exercise these cognitive skills.

We should also be clear in our own minds why we give such importance to these skills. Apart from philosophical and cultural reasons, the compelling practical argument is that organization makes ideas more portable and accessible – easier to convey, to reduce to essentials, to check, to locate. Organization is an intellectual power tool: once you have learned to use it, you cannot do without it.

There are many good exercises in published coursebooks, and a few more in this unit, but they generally have two drawbacks. On the one hand, they do not provide much motivation or rationale. Secondly, they are usually performed on other people's ideas, and an imaginative effort has to be made to bring these back to life before they can be reshaped. I feel that our business should be to give students practice in these skills while at the same time revealing

their *utility* in relation to their own ideas.

The game below introduces the main idea of the unit: that any sort of advance organizer gives shape and manageability to ideas.

Lead-in

A quick lead-in to the value of advance organizers is a version of Kim's Game. On a covered tray you have a number of objects (randomly arranged) which have a distinctive shape, material, colour or function – for example, two round things (a cork, a bottletop), two long thin things, three edible things and two things made of metal. Be careful not to overlap (e.g. a round thing made of metal).

Tell the group that they will see the objects for one minute only. Afterwards they will have to make a list of everything they can remember. Before exposing the tray, give half the class the (secret) instructions:

count
  – the round things   – the edible things
  – the long thin things   – the metal things.

Afterwards, score the two groups. On average, the 'organized' memorizers should have better scores than the 'disorganized' memorizers. Discuss how the memory task was lightened by this advance organizer and draw the moral that their compositions too will be more memorable if they are well and visibly organized.

This activity can be extended to producing reports on mini-meetings and group discussions and to listening and reading comprehension.

Follow-up

Discuss any ideas students have had for Tasks 2, 3 and 4 which differ from those given in the Key: students should be applauded if they have found convincing alternatives.

Reading text: The fun they had

Warm-up

Exchange reminiscences about primary schooldays – for example about:
 – the first day   – an awful teacher
 – a favourite teacher   – the most interesting lessons
 – a moment of shame   – the clothes you wore
 – the games you played   – getting hurt (mentally or
                              physically)

Record a few for future reference.

Read and discuss

Read *The fun they had* first. When is it set? (at least 150 years in the future). Is it a feasible picture? (This depends on whether they see education as individual development, shaped by technology, or as socialization.) Do they sympathize with Margie's nostalgia? Should learning be fun, or must it be hard work? Which way should education be going?

Bridge to assignment

Many people recall their schooling with a child's memory, and continue to receive education quite uncritically. The composition aims at a *critical* evaluation of one's own educational experience, past or present. Was/is it good enough? Why/Why not?

Suggest to students that a good starting point is to ask these questions about the reminiscences you started with. Give a few examples.

Planning work

If students opt for exam conditions for this last assignment, then they should start from cold, without any help. If not, use the texts as a lead-in, and then, to provide an advance organizer, get students to draw up a small table of best and worst educational experiences, now and in their childhood.

After getting some contributions, draw an arrow from Worst to Best and ask how things have changed, or how they could be expected to.

	Best experience	Worst experience
Now		
Then		

Marking

The last assignment should be marked applying all the criteria of language and composition, i.e. all those treated in Unit 3, together with style, layout and illustrative force. Your assessment will parallel the reader's evaluation (*q.v.*) and will also include linguistic accuracy and 'fluency' (which readers are not fully competent to assess).

Ask students to hand in their complete Record Sheet and also their first two assignments. On the basis of these, award a separate mark for progress during the course. It is worth emphasizing that this is the more important mark of the two.

KEY TO LANGUAGE TESTS

TEST A: Grammar/Structures

UNIT 1

a *information*   b *pieces of advice*
c *job/piece of work*

UNIT 2

The situation isn't so good. I **haven't done** very much of the course yet. I **had** some problems with the second unit: I **didn't understand** some of the points and I **couldn't** do one of the exercises. In the end I **asked** David to help me.

Anyway, I think **I've understood** it now and I expect I'll make better progress from now on.

UNIT 3

... They don't listen to **each other**, they only listen to **themselves**.

UNIT 4

No definite articles are necessary. Did you put any in?

UNIT 5

1 *may/might/could*   2 *might/could*
3 *may/may well/might*   4 *may/might*
5 *may/may well/might/will*
6 *might/would/will*
7 *may/may well/will*

N.B. You can use *could* for future possibility, but it is less versatile than *may/might*. It cannot be used in the following: a) with negatives, b) with *have to* or *be able to*, c) to distinguish between probabilities (*may well*), possibilities (*may*) and more remote possibilities (*might*).

UNIT 6

a *most people*   b *the majority of*
c *everyone*   d *Some/Some people think*

UNIT 7

I **have no** exams until June, so I **am** feeling very relaxed. My boyfriend **has** a new motorbike and we go out almost every evening. I expect I **will** regret it when June comes, but I **am** having a good time at the moment.

UNIT 8

a *however*   *on the other hand*
b *Though*   *Although*   *While*   *Whereas*

N.B. *On the contrary* is not used just to make a contrast, but to **say the opposite** of what has been said before. E.g. '*You'll get tired of it.*' '*On the contrary, I shall enjoy it*'/'*I have never been an enemy of the monarchy; on the contrary, I think monarchies are excellent institutions.*'

UNIT 9

the traffic problems   *the league's policy*
the problems of traffic   *the policy of the*
Michael's ideas   *league*
                            the world of work

UNIT 10

a *have to do with* OR
b *(got) to do with* OR
c *connected with*

TEST B: Vocabulary

UNIT 1

a *going*   b *on*   c *getting* (*in getting* is not wrong but is less usual)

UNIT 2

a X is **3 kilometres from** Y.
b That's **a long way** to walk.

UNIT 3

a 1 *known*   2 *met*   3 *meet*   4 *get to know*
b 1 *discover/find out*   2 *knew*   3 *know*
  4 *find out/discover*
  5 *found out/discovered*
  6 *knew (had found out/had discovered)*
  7 *find out/discover*

UNIT 4

allow us to   enable us to
make it possible (for us) to
permit us to

UNIT 5

a *in the last few months   in recent months*
of late   lately

b *nowadays   these days   at present*
at the present time

c *in the near future   in the next few months*
shortly

UNIT 6

a Rachel has *one son.*
b Marie and David are Lucy's *children.*
c They are *young people*, or (infrequently)
boys and girls.

UNIT 7

1 *emphasize/point out/stress/make it clear*
2 *certainly/undoubtedly/without question*

UNIT 8

a 1 *got married*   2 *been married*   3 *to*
4 *getting*
b 1 *was born*   2 *died*   3 *died*   4 *dead*

UNIT 9

Politicians go into **politics** not because they
want to put their **policies** into practice, but
because they feel at home in the **political** world.

Economists study **economics** and know all
about the **economic** forces that rule the world,
but they are not always **economical** with
money in ordinary life.

UNIT 10

I think Acceptable alternatives are:

To my mind   In my opinion
As I see it   I would say that
I feel that   I would suggest that
I agree that

Key to Units
UNIT 1
Language Preparation
Exercise 1

The following words and expressions can be
used with uncountables:

a little **rubbish**   a lot of **rubbish**
not much **rubbish**   very little **rubbish**
all **rubbish**   some **rubbish**   more **rubbish**
enough **rubbish**   plenty of **rubbish**

Exercise 2

a *some information*
b *piece of information*   **c** *some advice*
d *piece of advice*   **e** *advice*
f *pieces of advice*   **g** *equipment*
h *much/little equipment*
i *piece of equipment*   **j** *work*
k *piece of work*   **l** *pieces of work/jobs*

Exercise 5

a *for*   **b** *of*   **c** *on*   **d** *At*
e *no preposition*   **f** *in*   **g** *in*   **h** *for*   **i** *on*
j *at*

Exercise 6

Days of the week: Monday   Tuesday
Wednesday   Thursday   Friday   Saturday
Sunday

Months of the year: January   February
March   April   May   June   July   August
September   October   November   December

Writing Tutorial
Reading text

To interpret your answers, put a circle around
– the numbers you answered YES in the
questionnaire
– the letters of the sayings you selected.
Then see which box you fit into best, on the
next page.

If you do not fit into any box very well, you are probably a normal healthy human being!

UNWORLDLY	MATERIALIST				
Romantics, intellectuals, saints and charlatans	General	Thrifty housewife	Active manipulator	Anxious hoarder	Happy spender
1 15 18 19 26	4	2 6 13 20 22	5 8 10 17 21	9 11 14 16 23	3 7 12 24 25
a c f n o p	g l s	r t	v u w d j m x z	i y h	b e k q

UNIT 2
Language Preparation

Exercise 1

Only the narrative elements are given.

Dear Jo,
   Rolf visited us for a week in July – he seemed very tired, but that didn't stop him from working: he dug the garden and planted lots and lots of vegetables.

Dear Liz,
   I met Jackie on her way through from Hong Kong. She brought Jamie with her and we had a night out together – late, late very late.

Dear Sol,
   We were sorry you couldn't come to the wedding. It all went very well, but really there were too many people: we were exhausted afterwards.

Exercise 2

The narrative sequences are framed.

a I don't know **what's happened** to Alex these last few days. You know we've always said how mean he is and how uninterested in helping with the house. Well, it seems that he **has reformed.**

> On Friday he **offered** to do the shopping, then yesterday he **cleaned** the bathroom and **took** the rubbish out without being asked – and while he was out he **bought** a cake for tea!

We are all astonished and can't wait to see what happens next. The question is: why? We suspect that Irene has been talking to him.

b (From Australia) How are things with you? Many greetings from soggy Sydney. **It's been** a little wet for me, but I hope it will improve. Luckily I **haven't had** time to go to the beach yet.

> I **left** my driver's licence behind in England, but no problem – in half an hour I **had** a new one: and **there was** no queue, no delay. They **even smiled** at me! I might even say I **enjoyed** the experience.

   I **haven't seen** all the family yet – there are such a lot of them. Am working slowly down the list!

Exercise 3

a *a long way* b *a long way* c *away*
d *further (away)* e *(away) from* f *far*
g *a long way* h *far*

N.B. With reference to distance, *further* and *farther* are exactly the same in British English.

Exercise 4

a *to* b *of* c *to* d *no preposition* e *in*
f *no preposition* g *on* h *on* i *at* j *in*

Writing Tutorial

Task 1 Hot air Samples A, D and E
Something to say Samples B, C and F

UNIT 3
Language Preparation

Exercise 1

1 *each other*	2 *each other.*	3 *each other*
4 *each other*	5 *each other*	6 *themselves*
7 *each other*	8 *each other*	9 *himself*
10 *herself*	11 *themselves*	12 *each other*

Exercise 2

(The crossed out words refer to the task in Point Two.)

Romeo and Juliet were born into two families which hated ¹**each other** and were always fighting. They never spoke to ²**each other.**

Romeo and Juliet met ³~~each other~~ at a ball at Juliet's house (Romeo was not invited). They saw ⁴**each other** across the crowded room and fell in love ~~with ⁵each other~~ instantly. It was irresistible: they couldn't help ⁶**themselves.** They managed to meet ⁷~~each other~~ once or twice and got married secretly.

They wanted to run away together but they were separated ~~from ⁸each other~~. Romeo, thinking Juliet was dead, killed ⁹**himself** and Juliet, when she realized Romeo was dead, killed ¹⁰**herself** too.

Their families blamed ¹¹**themselves** for this tragedy and were finally reconciled ~~with ¹²each-other~~.

Exercise 3

a *got to know* b *meet/get to know* c *met*
d *know/get to know* e *get to know*
f *got to know* g *met* h *known*
i *know, find out* j *knows*

Exercise 4

a *for* b *to* c *no preposition*
d *no preposition* e *on* f *in* g *of* h *on*
i *in* j *no preposition*

Exercise 5

Prepositions and paper
- If you are talking about information in a publication which has several pages (a book, a newspaper, a brochure), you say it is **in** the publication.
- If you are talking about a page you usually use **on.**
- If you are talking about a point on the page (e.g. top, bottom) you use **at.**

Exercise 6

a *ceiling* b *briefly* c *achievement* d *receipt*
e *deceive* f *relieved* g *believe* h *thief*

UNIT 4
Language Preparation

Exercise 2

a The Constitution of the United States was written with ~~the~~ free trade principles in mind.
b Capitalism gives priority to ~~the~~ material things such as ~~the~~ cars, ~~the~~ houses, ~~the~~ clothes.
c The economic growth in America at that time resulted in a reduction in ~~the~~ inflation and ~~the~~ unemployment.
d He discovered in himself a great love for ~~the~~ nature and ~~the~~ animals.

Exercise 4

a *for* b *of* c *in* d *at* e *to*
f *no preposition* g *in* h *on* i *At* j *in*

Exercise 5

Prepositions and travel
- You always go/travel/fly **to** a place, whether it is a country or a town.

Prepositions and composition
- Things consist/are composed/are made up **of** parts and elements.

Exercise 6

In fact there is no need for commas at all in these sentences. Commas are *optional* in sentences c and d:

c He thinks he is sick and he says he is sick, but I have the feeling⬚, on the whole⬚, that he is perfectly all right.

d There is no doubt that animals affect people in many ways. It is clear⬚, for example⬚, that having a pet often improves people's health.

UNIT 5
Language Preparation

Exercise 1

A What are Peter's chances of getting the job, would you say?

B Well, in fact, **Peter might not/may not/may well not** apply.

A Really?

B Yes. It seems he's been approached by another firm and he **might/may** take that job instead.

A But **he may not/he might not?**

B That's right.

A And Jack? What are his chances? He's applied, hasn't he?

B Oh, yes. Well, it depends on who else applies. If they find someone really excellent, **Jack may well not** even get an interview.

A But **they may/might not** be able to find anyone that good.

B Well, in that case the Board **may** appoint Jack. Or **they just might** leave the vacancy open.

A So **we might not** have anyone in the post?

B We **may well** not.

A Or **they may/might** put Jack in as a temporary manager?

B They **may/might/may well.**

Exercise 3

a *in the last few days*   b *lately*
c *in recent years*   d *of late* (quite formal)
e *not long ago*   f *these days*   g *Nowadays*
h *At present*   i *at the present time/moment*
j *in the near future*   k *shortly* (quite formal)
l *in the next few months*
N.B. You can say 'in the next/last few months/ days/weeks' but you can't say 'in the next months', etc.

Exercise 5

a *for*   b *in* or no preposition   c *in*   d *out*
e *in*   f *on*   g *at*   h *but*   i *on*   j *by*

Exercise 6

Prepositions and time
● **At** is used for points in time (the hour, the moment, the present). **In** is used for periods of time starting from now (**in** *the next few months*, **in** *a few minutes*).

Prepositions are not needed
● usually with movements to and from *home* – *go home, get home, arrive home, leave home* (but in British English you need a preposition when you are **at** *home*)
● with *ask, answer, tell* – that is, with the *person* you ask, answer or tell.

Exercise 7

a *happier*   b *employed*   c *daily*   d *copying*
e *enjoyable*   f *studying*   g *studied*   h *dying*
i *supplied*   j *supplying*   k *lying*   l *paid*

These are the rules:
1 The **y** at the end of a word normally changes to an **i** when you add a suffix, e.g. *happier, supplied*.
2 But if the suffix starts with **i** (like -**ing**), then you keep the **y** because it is impossible to have two letter **i**'s together. So we have *studying* and *copying*.
3 To avoid having two **i**s together, you must also sometimes change an **i** to a **y**, for example in *dying* and *lying*.
4 If there is a vowel before the **y** (e.g. *enjoy, employ*) then you do not change the **y** to an **i**
   . . .
5 . . . except in four cases: *daily, said, paid* and *laid*.

Writing Tutorial

Task 1

Composition A **Reverse indentation**. The composition is divided into paragraphs but they are not indented correctly.

Composition B **No paragraphing** at all.

Composition C **No indentation** and there are too many **one-sentence paragraphs**.

Composition D **No indentation**. The composition is divided into paragraphs, but it could probably do with some more.

Task 2

Order of paragaphs in article on asparagus:

5 asparagus in literature
1 the medical value of asparagus
4 asparagus with other food
3 how to cook asparagus
6 what kind of dressing goes with asparagus + a story to illustrate this
2 a recipe for asparagus

Task 3

Paragraph 1 The image
Paragraph 2 The reality
Paragraph 3 How the image and the reality interact/come together

Task 4

We would suggest a new paragraph at 'A first lady is always busy'. Another would be possible at 'Another reason . . .': this is certainly a new subject, but the very short paragraph that would result would interrupt the flow of the composition.

Task 5

We would suggest new paragraphs begin at 'I do not agree with this opinion' and 'I think that . . .' – but there are other possibilities.

UNIT 6
Language Preparation

Exercise 1

The problem is that Carlo is talking about old people in general, but because he is using *the* Neil thinks he is referring to a specific group of old people.

Exercise 2

Everyone avoided the old factory. Some said that it was haunted: that the night watchman who had been killed there still walked around it at night when **everything** was dark. Not **everyone** agreed with this story. In particular, Joe thought it was rubbish, and said so. But in spite of **everything** he said, he was just like **everyone else** – he too never went near the factory.

Exercise 4

a *people* b *children, children*
c *young people/teenagers*
d *sons, daughters* (or two *boys* and two *girls*) e *children*
f *children, teenagers/young people* g *child, son/boy* h *children* i *grandchildren*
j *daughters/girls, sons/boys* k *niece*
l *grandchild/grandson, nephew*.

Exercise 5

a *out* b *but* c *off* d *no preposition*
e *to* f *on* g *for* h *at* i *in* j *on*

Exercise 6

Prepositions and the mass media
Information in print is usually **in** a book, a newspaper, a magazine, a brochure. You use **in** where there is a story or narrative – **in** a story, **in** a report – and so also **in** a film. But for TV and radio the usual preposition is **on** – **on** TV, **on** the radio, **on** the screen, **on** Channel 5.

Exercise 7

The possibilities are colon(:), semi-colon (;), dash (–) and full-stop (.). Not all are possible in each case (consult your teacher or a reference book for more information). The choice is often personal, so the answers here are in what we think is the order of popularity. For example, in the first position we think most people would put a colon; some would put a dash; some would use a semi-colon and a few would use a full-stop.

1 Colon, dash, semi-colon, full-stop
2 Semi-colon, dash, colon, full-stop 3 Dash
4 Dash 5 Full-stop, semi-colon, colon or dash

Exercise 8

1 Full-stop, colon, dash, semi-colon
2 Dash, semi-colon, colon 3 Dash
4 Colon, dash, semi-colon, full-stop

Writing Tutorial

Task 1

1 A is more convergent, B is more divergent.
2 Example A is already half planned.
3 The first idea in Example A was that trees are efficient and essential.
The second idea was about types of tree.
The third idea was about dangers to trees.
The fourth idea was that we must do something to protect trees.

Task 3

Two other main ideas that seem to emerge from Example B are:

1 *The importance of trees and the need to protect and care for them.* This takes in the points about the Amazon, countries' tree policies, forest police, deforestation and cities looking after trees.
2 *Trees in the writer's life.* This covers climbing trees as a child, trees the writer has planted, trees in countries where the writer has lived, favourite trees, and possibly the idea of the forest meaning life.

You may have found different connections.

UNIT 7
Language Preparation

Exercise 1

A long time ago there **were no** cars. We **cannot** say that there **were no** accidents in those days, as it was always possible for a cart or a chariot to hit something or somebody, but at least there **was no** pollution.

Nowadays, by contrast, everyone **has** a car and as a result it is **no longer** possible to walk in the streets or to breathe clean air. Moreover, air pollution **does not** only affect people: **it is** also damaging the stone and metal of buildings and statues. For example, our cathedral's walls are black and dirty, but the cost of cleaning them is enormous. There was a magnificent bronze equestrian statue in the main square of our town but now **it has** been removed for restoration. Possibly **we will** never see it again. But the statue is lucky. For the little stone faces on the cathedral walls there **is no** remedy: **they have** already lost their noses, and this has

happened in just the last twenty years.

I **do not have** a car myself, and I feel that I **am** being sacrificed for the people who have. Before my nose disappears as well, I want to say 'NO MORE CARS! NO MORE POLLUTION! LET ME BREATHE!'

Exercise 2

This is one possible version. Yours may be different.

I would like to point out that Mr Longbotham has always been **remarkably** friendly, and has **certainly** helped us to settle into our new home. When we arrived in the street, we did not have any furniture **at all** and Mr Longbotham went to a **great deal** of trouble to find some for us. If it was not for him, we would **undoubtedly** still be sitting on the floor. He has done us a **considerable number** of favours and **I want to stress that** we will always be **extremely** grateful to him. So I find it very difficult **indeed** to believe that he is a mass murderer.

Exercise 3

a *for* b *at* c *with* d *in*
e *no preposition* f *no preposition* g *in*
h *In* i *in* j *no preposition*

Exercise 4

Prepositions and needs/desires
● The nouns *demand*, *wish*, *desire* and *need* all take the preposition **for** (*need* also sometimes takes **of**).
Prepositions and futility
● *It's no use . . .*, *It's no good . . .*, have the **-ing** form and no preposition. *There's no point . . .* has **in + -ing**, or sometimes no preposition.

Exercise 5

1 *choices* 2 *choose* 3 *chose* 4 *choice*
5 *Choosing* 6 *choice* 7 *chose*

Writing Tutorial

Task 1

The differences between Versions A and B:

1 **Words** 'I find . . .' and 'I feel . . .' (instead of, for example, 'I really hate') give a tone of less emotion and more judgement.
2 **Sentences** The sentences are generally longer and more complex and there are no rhetorical questions.
3 **Organization** There is less repetition and the points are in a logical order – opinion leading to conclusion.

Task 2

A1 spoken English style
A2 semi-formal style
B1 semi-formal style
B2 spoken English style

Task 4

1 **Problem** A sort of *tautology*. The addicts do not stop doping themselves *by* renouncing drugs: they stop doping themselves *when* they renounce drugs.

Improvement *In this Centre drug addicts are helped to stop doping themselves*, **or** *In this Centre drug addicts are helped to renounce drugs for ever.*

2 **Problem** *Over-generalization*. It does not apply to all models – it is unlikely that it even applies to most models.

Improvement *Unlike ordinary people, models often have exciting lives and often change their husbands or boyfriends.*

3 **Problem** *Internal contradiction*. If it was a desert island then it was not inhabited.

Improvement *Robinson Crusoe landed on a desert island*, **or** *Robinson Crusoe landed on an island inhabited only by savages.*

4 **Problem** *Sloppy wording*. A career is not a job, so it can't be 'one of the best jobs'.
Improvement *We often think that we would all like to have glamorous careers.*

5 **Problem** *Mixed metaphor*. This is nice. Do they have horizontal doors? In the ceiling?

Improvement *In this company there are always opportunities for those who want to rise to higher positions.*

6 **Problem** *Tautology*. Of course he tells lies. He is dishonest.

Improvement *I know he tells lies*, **or** *I know he is dishonest.*

7 **Problem** Another *internal contradiction*, and also a sort of *mixed metaphor*. The key can't be in your pocket because your pocket is empty. In this case the original sentence is so funny it seems a pity to change it.

Improvement *The key to the problem is lack of money.*

8 **Problem** *Over-generalization*. Not *all* young people, not *all* their lives.

Improvement *A large proportion of young people spend a great part of their lives looking in vain for jobs.*

UNIT 8
Language Preparation

Exercise 4

a 1 *to*   2 *getting*   3 *get*   4 *get*   5 *are*
b 1 *born*   2 *died*   3 *born*   4 *dead*
c *married*   d 1 *Dead*   2 *dead*   3 *dead*
4 *dead*

Exercise 6

a *up*   b *with*   c *for*   d *about*   e *in*
f *to*   g *On*   h *By*   i *in*   j *on*

Exercise 7

Prepositions and change
The preposition which goes with nouns of change (*change, improvement, deterioration, decrease, rise, drop, fall, alteration*) is usually **in**.

Exercise 8

a Archimedes is said to have cried *Eureka*! when he suddenly discovered a scientific principle about the displacement of water (they say he was in his bath at the time).
b 'I have a dream' is the theme of Martin Luther King's most famous speech about racial equality.
c 'In the beginning was the Word' are the first words of St. John's Gospel, in the Bible.
d Lady Macbeth in her dreams tries to wash imaginary blood from her hands, crying 'Out, damned spot!'

e It was the philospher Descartes who said 'I think, therefore I am'.

f The phrase 'the wine-dark sea' is used many times by Homer in the *Odyssey*.

g 'She loves me, yeah, yeah, yeah' is the refrain of one of the Beatles' best-known songs.

h '*Carpe diem*', originally from a poem by Horace, has come to stand for a whole philosophy of life.

i 'I can resist everything except temptation' says Lady Windermere in a play by Oscar Wilde. Many attribute this quotation directly to Oscar Wilde.

j 'Life, liberty and the pursuit of happiness' are the 'inalienable rights' of man mentioned in the American Declaration of Independence.

Writing Tutorial

Task 1

1 examples   2 examples/illustrations
3 an illustration/quotation
4 particulars/details   5 an example

Task 2

Only the examples are shown:

... Michelle Pfeiffer, for example, began by shooting TV commercials and when she entered films was immediately type-cast as the dumb blonde and could not get any other kind of part.

... (arms and equipment manufacturers and dealers, builders, ministry employees, career officers and so on).

... McDonalds has arrived in Moscow, we all watch 'Dallas', Coca-Cola is replacing wine and beer and everybody smokes Marlboro.

... the word 'OK' is universal.

... As for washing dishes and cleaning toilets, cooking and 'becoming a man' ...,

Task 5

There are many possibilities for this exercise. Here are some:

1 Every evening she waters **the geraniums and the climbing roses on her balcony.**

2 She always wears **Armani jeans and Chanel suits.**

3 He steals **pencils, sweets, little notebooks and small toys** from shops.

4 The car was dirty and full of **old newspapers, wrappers from bars of chocolate, used paper tissues, rubber bands, shopping lists and discarded plastic carrier bags.**

5 He wastes his money on **cigarettes and playing video games.**

6 When you do military service, you have to **wash dishes, sweep floors, peel potatoes, iron clothes, cook and serve food,** and so on.

Task 7

1 **Paragraph   Idea**

   1 Until recently women were not free.

   2 Now they can legally do everything men can do.

   3 But this 'freedom' is not completely real.

   4 Women must make this freedom a reality.

   5 We need to have a balanced world.

2 **Paragraph   Illustration**

   1 The story of the film 'The Colour Purple'

   2 Examples: study, vote, work plus idea of a girl child as a disgrace

   3 There are few women managers and TV journalists

   4 Example: women's centres

   5 (Paragraph 5 has no illustrations.)

UNIT 9
Language Preparation

Exercise 1

a *the sign of Capricorn*
b *Her teddy bear's foot*
c *The windows of the houses*
d *The question of Palestine*
(**N.B.** The question *concerns* Palestine; it doesn't belong to Palestine.)
e *Scotland's position*
f *Our team of experts*
g *the ecstasy of flight*
h *The world of finance*
i *the problems of pollution*
j *Children's rights*

Exercise 2

	ECONOMICS	POLITICS
The people are	*economists*	*politicians*
The plans they have are	–	*policies*
The aspect of the country is the	*economy*	*politics*
The adjectives are	*economic*	*political*
	economical	–
The adverbs are	*economically*	*politically*
or	*in economic terms*	*in political terms*
	from an economic point of view	*from a political point of view*

Notes:
- *Politics* and *economics* are singular, like *mathematics*.
- *Economic* relates to the economy and to economics; *economical* means cheap, money-saving. (Not much used when talking about economics.)
- Notice the pronunciation of these words. The stress changes: **pol**itics   po**li**tical   poli**ti**cians   eco**nom**ics   eco**nom**ical   e**con**omist

Exercise 3

a *politicians*   b *economy, political, economic*   c *economical*   d *economic, economic*   e *economists, policies*   f *politics, economics, politics*   g *policy*   h *economically, politically*

Exercise 4

a *at*   b *in*   c *after*   d *by*   e *from*
f *about/with*   g *to*   h *no preposition*
i *By*   j *as*

Exercise 5

Prepositions and capacities/attitudes
- Apart from *bad* **at**, *good* **at** etc., the prepositions with adjectives like *interested* (**in**) and *keen* (**on**) seem to be quite arbitrary and have to be learnt separately.

Prepositions and generalizing
- Expressions meaning 'generally' are **in** *general*, **on** *the whole* and **by** *and large*.

Exercise 6

bring	brought	mean	meant
buy	bought	read	read
catch	caught	teach	taught
deal	dealt	think	thought
fight	fought	win	won
hear	heard		

Writing Tutorial

Task 2

Ending 1 just continues the subject.
Ending 2 wraps up the whole composition.
Ending 3 introduces a new subject: love.

Ending 2 is the best ending.

Task 3

The original ending was:

> The question is whether it is better to have had the glamour and lost it, or never to have had it. I don't know the answer.

This wraps up the two main ideas of the composition nicely.

Task 4

Sentence
2	Stowton
3	Mac and Julia
4	Julia's family
5	Julia's family's factory
6–7	The biscuits

Task 5

Line C is the one which maintains the subject.
Lines A and B ramble away from it.

Task 6

The digression is:

*Becoming a model is difficult because you have
to have particular qualities; for example, you
must be quite tall, thin and pretty.*

This has nothing to do with the glamorous
image of a model, or the unglamorous reality.

UNIT 10
Language Preparation

Exercise 1

(**N.B.** *Your answers may be different.*)

a Petrol and coal are both fossil fuels.
b A lot/Quite a lot/Not very much/Nothing at
all.
c Nothing at all – unless you can think of some
connection, e.g. *roast chicken is tied up with
string.*
d An iron used to be made entirely from iron.
Now irons are made from steel and plastic.
e A great deal. You may have thought of the
question of oxygen in the atmosphere, or
rare species, or the rights of the Amazon
Indians.

Exercise 4

a *of, of* b *In* c *on* d *in* e *with*
f *To* g *As* h *in* i *with* j *With*

Exercise 5

a **Prepositions and intention**
  ● by and on. *on purpose*, **by** *chance* and **by**
    accident.
b **Prepositions and responsibility**
  ● with: *deal* **with** and *cope* **with**; the other
    two are *look* **after** and *take care* **of.** There
    is no general rule.

Exercise 6

Can you evaluate a school's performance by its
examination results? This is the interesting
question raised by the British Government's
decision to publish schools' examination
results and rank the schools in a 'league table'.
There was a furious reaction from some
schools. Mrs Jaggers, headmistress of Subeaton
Comprehensive School, said, 'The government
is out of touch. It is quite clear that their
priorities are not the same as ours. Results
depend on the areas the schools are in and on
the local councils' policies as much as on each
school's efforts.' Mrs Jaggers' school's results
are about average.

Some interesting facts emerged from the
'league table'. One school's performance
appeared much better than the others (the
others'), but it was discovered that this school
was actually sending its students out to a
tutorial agency for extra lessons.

N.B. *Others* has an apostrophe if the meaning
is *other (schools') performances*. If the meaning
is *other performances* then it does not need an
apostrophe.

Writing Tutorial

Task 2

1/2 Here is one way the points could be
grouped and ordered:

The extent of dialect use
  1 there are many dialects
  7 dialect is alive in my town

Threats to dialects
Problems
  2 they create problems of comprehension
Loss of use
  5 young people can't speak dialects any more
Negative attitudes
  3 people laugh at dialect-users
  9 people despise dialect-speakers

Dialects should be encouraged
  4 dialects should be kept alive
  6 dialects should be encouraged
10 we should keep dialects alive
because
  8 dialects are important in national history
11 they are part of our culture

Task 3

In fact there are about five main ideas – see if you agree with our list:

Idea

1 The way exams are organized.
2 The *facts* of the writer's situation (what exams she has to take and when).
3 The writer's difficulties and the reasons for them, i.e. her personal limitations and her lack of time.
4 Her feelings about her examination situation (fear, frustration, anxiety).
5 The result: a critical situation.

Task 4

Notes for an essay on problems at the university

a **Administration**
   ● Language teachers should have their contracts in time so that language classes can start on time.

b **Personal development**
   ● The University is just a degree factory. It does not really train students for jobs or help them to grow personally.
   ● New students don't know how to study and there is no one to help them. They need tutorial advice.
   ● The University should help students to make their own choices and decisions so that they can become complete adults and move easily into the working world.

c **Admissions policy**
   ● Students should do an entry test to see if they are good enough to be admitted to courses. Attendance can still be optional, as there are students who live far away.
   ● The University should not have too many students for the places it has. If too many sign on, there is little contact between students and teachers.

d **Curriculum**
   ● Language teaching must prepare for examinations. Teachers should have similar criteria for every session and year.
   ● The studies are too theoretical and unrelated to real life – they don't prepare students for work.

e **Social life**
   ● Students are isolated from each other.
   ● It is also difficult for students to meet other students and discuss things.

f **Geography/layout**
   ● A university should have a compact campus, and not be scattered all over the city. This makes it difficult to study properly.

g **Links with the outside world**
   ● The University should provide work experience opportunities.
   ● The University has few contacts with the world of work.
   ● Jobs require experience and it's very difficult to get experience. Only people whose parents have the right sort of contacts can get work experience.
   ● A modern university should organize international meetings and cultural exchanges.
   ● The University should have contact with museums, art galleries, theatres, famous companies, etc.